Girl for Sale

Girl for Sale

The truth from the girl trafficked
and abused by the Oxford sex ring

LARA MCDONNELL

EBURY
PRESS

1 3 5 7 9 10 8 6 4 2

Ebury Press, an imprint of Ebury Publishing
20 Vauxhall Bridge Road
London SW1V 2SA

Ebury Press is part of the Penguin Random House group of companies
whose addresses can be found at global.penguinrandomhouse.com

Penguin
Random House
UK

First published by Ebury Press in 2015

www.eburypublishing.co.uk

A CIP catalogue record for this book is available from the British Library

ISBN 9780091957810

Printed and bound by CPI Group (UK) Ltd, Croydon, CR0 4YY

Penguin Random House is committed to a sustainable future for
our business, our readers and our planet. This book is made from
Forest Stewardship Council® certified paper.

To my son. I hope you understand how special you are.

Contents

Prologue: No escape   1

Chapter one: A family snapshot   5

Chapter two: Brief sanctuary   17

Chapter three: Moving on   27

Chapter four: Forever families   39

Chapter five: Alone   53

Chapter six: The kid who waited   71

Chapter seven: Mum   83

Chapter eight: School's out   97

Chapter nine: Out of control   119

Chapter ten: Egyptian Mo   129

Chapter eleven: Payback   147

Chapter twelve: Lost girl   157

Chapter thirteen: Skin trade   175

Chapter fourteen: Sam the Rapist   189

Chapter fifteen: Lara vs Lauren   199

Chapter sixteen: Human traffic   211

Chapter seventeen: A hope   227

Chapter eighteen: Noah   239

Chapter nineteen: Choose life   257

Chapter twenty: Operation Bullfinch   267

Chapter twenty-one: The trial   281

Epilogue: Blameless   301

Acknowledgements   309

Prologue

NO ESCAPE

The shrill ringtone made me jump, even though I was expecting the text. I didn't have to read it; I knew the gist of what it said and who had sent it. As soon as I heard the noise and saw the screen of my phone light up my heart began to beat faster. Tension, anxiety and fear threatened to overwhelm me and I started to breathe faster as I reached for the handset.

'B here in 10. Friends here.'

Six short words. My instructions. I didn't need any more detail than what was written on the screen. The person who sent it was careful enough to be vague – he didn't want to leave any evidence. I knew exactly what was required of me and I knew I couldn't refuse. I shivered and tried to calm myself; my head swam as I attempted to come to terms with what I was about to do.

I sat down on the pretty floral duvet cover on my bed and tried to pull myself together.

'You've done it before – it'll be over in a few hours. The drugs will help,' I told myself.

I hugged my knees and rocked back and forth. My bedroom was warm and cosy. It should have been my sanctuary but there was nowhere I felt safe.

My bed was clean and comfortable. The bookshelf was full of my favourite stories and a sketch pad lay open on my desk. Bradley from the pop band S Club 7 gazed down at me from a poster on the wall. It was a typical young girl's room but I was not a typical young girl.

The place I was being summoned to could not have been more different from the room I was leaving. The squalid flat was just a short walk away from the three-storey Victorian house I lived in but it might as well have been on another planet. It was a crack den. The drug fumes always stung my nostrils when I walked in. They smelled like burning plastic and they sparked a craving in me. The drugs numbed me. I knew that, as soon as those fumes filled my lungs, what followed – the men and the abuse – would be more bearable.

Downstairs my mum was cooking dinner. The smell of homemade casserole filled the house. But I had no appetite – I hadn't eaten a proper meal in weeks. I started to work out how I was going to leave the house. I had no keys. Mum wouldn't allow me a set – it was her way of trying to keep tabs on me. She was frantic with worry. I disappeared on an almost-daily basis and always after a text message. She didn't know the half of what was going on; she didn't know about the drugs and the men and I wasn't about to tell her.

I was ashamed and I was also scared. How had I let myself get into the position I was in? My life was a complete mess.

I didn't know who I could trust or who my friends were; all I knew was that, as soon as the texts came through, I needed to get out.

The man who sent them called it work. It was my job. I belonged to him and I did what he told me to do. He gave me alcohol and a constant supply of drugs; in return I did as I was told. I was there to service his customers.

It hadn't always been that way. Once, I believed I could trust him. I believed he was my friend but, increasingly, he terrified me. I knew that if I refused what he asked then he would hunt me down and he would hurt me. It made no difference to him whether the police or social workers knew. As far as he was concerned, they couldn't do anything.

I reached under my bed and felt around for the screwdriver I used for breaking the lock on the window. My hands were shaking as I wedged it between the window and the frame and popped open the catch that held it shut. Slowly I pushed the window open. Mum was still cooking downstairs. The sound of the crockery and the fan on the oven masked the sound of the window sliding open. I had broken out many times before and nimbly climbed through the open space, onto the security light outside and jumped down into the garden.

As I did so the light came on. I saw Mum look up and stare out of the kitchen window.

'Lara!' she cried. 'Where are you going?'

But I was gone. There was no way she was going to stop me. It was dark and the cold night air hit me as I ran off. I was wearing only a hoodie and a pair of jeans. Other clothes would be provided for me where I was going. I would be made to wear the tarty underwear the men insisted on. The thought of it made my skin crawl but I didn't have a choice.

My phone trilled again. I glanced at the screen as I ran over the bridge. The spires of Oxford University shone in the distance.

'Where r u?'

'On the way,' I texted back hurriedly.

I rounded the corner of the estate and a gang of menacing-looking teenagers loitering there eyed me suspiciously. As I hurried past they said nothing.

The door was open when I arrived and I walked into the dirty main room. A stained sofa was placed in the middle of the room in front of a widescreen TV. The air was thick with crack fumes. Mohammed was waiting.

'Where the fuck have you been?' he hissed, his eyes dark and bloodshot.

'I… I… I had to get out of the house,' I stuttered.

He nodded towards the small, cluttered bedroom.

'Get in there and get that lot on,' he ordered. Through the door I could see underwear laid out on the bed. It was cheap and tacky adult lingerie.

Two men were sitting on the sofa behind Mohammed. Their eyes followed me as I walked into the room.

As I closed the door behind me I tried to understand how my life had become the misery it was. I was a slave, I was sold – I was just 13.

Chapter one

A FAMILY SNAPSHOT

My birth mother stares out of the photograph with empty eyes. The picture has been taped together with Sellotape. I ripped it in half several years ago in a fit of anger.

In the shot, she is holding me. It was taken when I was just a few months old. I'm dressed in a grubby babygro that had faded long before the photo was taken. A sun hat is plonked on my head. I am sitting on her knee. Her hands are holding me, but not supporting me; my head lolls uncomfortably to one side. She stares vacantly at the camera, disinterested.

She is Theresa Jenkins – Terri. Born in the Northwest of England, she was adopted as soon as she was born. From what I know, her parents were very young when they had her and both were alcohol dependent. When Terri was born the kind of child protection procedures that we have in place today did not exist, so I can only imagine her parents must have been in no fit state to raise a child for her to be taken away from them.

But I don't call Terri 'Mum'. I used to when I was little but, as I got older, I started to realise that Mum is a title you earn, it doesn't get handed to you automatically.

Terri was 42 when she died. She had seven children. Two were not with my birth father, Shane Long. The eldest in my family is a girl, and her name is Isobel. I have never met her – she was adopted before I was born. Until I was eight, I knew nothing of her existence. In all, including half brothers and sisters, I have 11 siblings because Shane had children from a previous marriage. I have never met them either and I don't remember Shane ever visiting them. Our family was broken long before I came along and my birth parents' attitude to parental responsibility was non-existent.

The photograph tells me everything I need to know about my links with Terri. She is expressionless and detached from me, the baby on her lap, and from whatever else is going on around her. It looks as if I have been placed there against her will. Her body language is screaming, 'Take this thing away from me.' Any normal mother in a similar situation would be swollen with pride, eager to show off her little bundle of joy. They would be looking at the child in front of them and cooing or nuzzling up to her rosy cheeks. But Terri looks awkward; she is squirming away from me. It's the same in every photo I have of us together; she always looks detached and empty. She is devoid of love, affection and motherly pride. Her gaze is always somewhere else. In all the pictures I have seen of her with her children, the pose is the same: we are just plonked on her knee, like a succession of dolls. There is no intimacy; she does not cuddle up.

No one really remembers their early years entirely. We patch together a story of how we grew up through photos, snatches of memory and things we are told by our families. Some of my memories are vivid, others enhanced by reports on me that I have read over the years in a thick file passed between different agencies.

What happens in those early years of any child's life is vital. From birth to toddler and pre-school, those events form the way we see the world and inform our ideas about attachment and about relationships. All I remember is fear, violence and pain. Terri was a drunk and a junkie, Shane was a violent monster – the few memories I do have of them revolve around beatings and bloodshed.

Terri had long dark hair and a crooked nose. She wasn't an attractive lady by any means. She didn't look after herself; she never wore nice clothes, did her hair or wore make-up. She looked like an abused woman, which is what she was. She looked haunted; she had a hard life that shaped her features. Even when attempting a smile (which wasn't very often), she looked pained. In the few years I lived with Terri, her physical condition deteriorated sharply. I know now it was the crack cocaine and the heroin she was hooked on. As well as the photo of her holding me as a baby, I also have one of her with me, aged four. In those short years she has aged a decade: her eyes are puffy, her nose and cheeks purple with cracked blood vessels. Her complexion is sallow and pale. In the older photo she is 31 but she looks like a woman in her fifties. She had very bad teeth; I assume that was the drinking and the smoking (she was a very heavy smoker and always had a cough). She was overweight and had given up caring about herself long before she had kids, which she had in quick succession.

Shane looked like a criminal. The only photo I have of him is from a story on a news website reporting that he had been jailed for beating women. It didn't surprise me that he'd attacked women, or that the report went on to state that he had been aggressive to a child and one of the victims needed hospital treatment. What did surprise me was that he was described as a father. Like Terri, that was a title he never earned from me.

In the accompanying picture he looked evil. He had been married before he met Terri but they themselves never tied the knot. Unlike Terri, Shane made an effort with his appearance: he showered and attempted to slick back his black hair. As a child, I remember him as a giant, a tall aggressive ogre. His voice was very deep, with a Northern accent.

I was born in 1992 in North Staffs Hospital. My birth name was Lauren Long. I have since discovered that I weighed just 5lb when I was born and that Terri never had a scan or a check-up during her pregnancy. I was a very poorly newborn, but I guess I was lucky as some of my siblings were born with meningitis. I'm not sure why they were born with it, but I'm sure the poor conditions we lived in did not help. All I had to deal with was a dangerously low birth weight and foetal alcohol syndrome, which I developed because Terri drank throughout her pregnancy. My social services records show that she never had any antenatal care. My parents were both smokers. I have no reason to believe they gave up or reduced their intake during pregnancy, and from birth I had problems breathing, later diagnosed as asthma; also eczema and heart murmurs.

We lived in a rundown town in Staffordshire. Nondescript, it was full of council houses that all looked the same. Unemployment was high, aspirations low. I lived there with Terri, Shane, my older brother Jayden, older sister Kirsten and younger brothers, Harry and Jamie. I don't remember Terri working but then again I don't remember any of the neighbours working either.

Shane went out each day in his yellow van – I think he was involved in some sort of building work. Terri stayed at home with us children and drank herself into a stupor until he returned and beat her; usually because she was drunk. She became quite good at pretending to be sober but Shane always knew. She attempted to hide her empties round the house, behind bits of card, in cupboards and drawers, and became increasingly frantic as the day wore on, worrying about the next beating. It was a very abusive relationship, and Shane did nothing to hide the brutality and cruelty from us children.

We lived in squalor. The council house we called home was disgusting – dirty, damp, smelly and dark. From the outside, it was a featureless brick block with a scrubby front garden and a yard at the back. There was an old disused toilet outside. Everything about it was grey, grubby and depressing. It was the worst-kept property on a rough street in a rundown estate. Terri took no pride in it and Shane only appeared to flit in and out long enough to beat the mother of his kids.

Inside, the kitchen cupboards that were once white had long since turned brown, stained with grease and nicotine. There was rarely food in them. The oven was filthy and hardly ever used. In the lounge, there was a threadbare, grey carpet and a dull-coloured sofa. The curtains were dirty bits of material hung against windows that were smeared with dirt.

Upstairs there was a bathroom and one bedroom with a double bed in it. We all shared the same room and the same bed – I don't remember Shane ever sleeping there with us; I assume he was often out or asleep on the sofa. The bedroom floor was covered in the same grey carpet as the lounge and was strewn with dirty clothes. There were no comforts; nothing about the place that was welcoming: it was a house but it certainly wasn't a family home. I remember thinking it looked like a horror house, something you would see in a scary movie.

My memories of that place are thankfully limited because I don't have happy memories of early childhood at all. I remember in bursts: I remember drinking water out of shoes when there were no cups or glasses, the taste of leather in my mouth. I don't remember family meals together, but Terri must have cooked occasionally because I recall Shane once throwing a fork at her in the kitchen because he didn't like what he had been served up (it missed and hit my younger brother, Jamie, instead). I don't remember going out as a family, ever. There was no TV. I don't remember any toys. Most of the time we weren't dressed; we ran around in nappies that were usually heavy with excrement and urine and hung around our knees. What clothes we did have we shared; we

10

grabbed what was lying around. Sometimes the boys would wear the girls' clothes and vice versa. In another photo I have, Harry is a toddler and dressed in grubby girls' clothes. I remember Shane once tried to drown me in the bath. He was very drunk and was holding me under the water. Jayden came and hit him with a dustpan; that's when the police came. I can't remember who called them, it was usually Jayden or a neighbour. They wrapped me in a towel and took me out to their car. I remember feeling cold all the time. Winters were cruel and we would huddle together in the bed, trying to keep out the damp and the cold.

Then there were the mice. The place was infested with them – they were drawn to the filth. I saw them at night when the lights of a passing car lit up the bedroom. They would be caught, momentarily, in silhouette at the end of the bed, their oily bodies scurrying for cover. I tried to pretend they weren't there and hid under the dirty bed sheets or closed my eyes and pressed my face into one of my siblings' backs. In the silence, I could hear them run across the floor. To me it seemed like there were hundreds of them.

Christmases were not full of laughter and warmth. We didn't have a tree, although one year Shane hung a tree-shaped car air freshener up in the lounge as a sick joke. Presents were rare. On one occasion, when I was about three years old, I was given a pretty pink Barbie watch for Christmas. I loved it, it was the first possession I remember and I would wear it everywhere, even to bed. Then, one night, I made the mistake of taking it off and placing it on the floor before I went to sleep. In the morning the straps and the cheap plastic surround had been chewed by the rodents we shared our house with. Heartbroken, I received no sympathy.

The best Christmas I can remember in that house was the one when Shane arrived home with dogs as presents. I must have been three. I loved animals and it was magical, not only to have the pets but to have some sort of affection shown to us. It was Christmas Day and we were summoned downstairs to the lounge. Already I had heard the scampering, whimpering and barking before I opened the door and almost didn't want to believe it in case it wasn't true. I have no idea where the dogs came from but I have my suspicions: they weren't puppies. It was snowing outside and just for a moment everything was perfect. My sister and I shared Brandy, a long-haired golden retriever. Shane got the boys a mongrel, Mitch, to share, and he kept a Staffordshire Bull Terrier called Tyson – a vile creature – for himself.

For the next few weeks we were enthralled by our new pets. We'd play with them in the garden and take them for walks. Shane showed more affection to his status dog than he did to his wife and children – I suppose it boosted the hard man image he carefully maintained.

One afternoon, after we'd had the dogs for a while, I heard a commotion in the garden and looked out the window to see Tyson attacking Mitch. Jayden was screaming and trying to drag him off his dog. There was blood everywhere. The Staffie was ripping poor Mitch apart, continually snapping at its throat with its powerful jaws. The mongrel's injuries were so bad that it died there and then in the yard. Tyson was subsequently destroyed.

Home was a hellhole, no matter whether you were a kid or an animal.

There was no routine. We went to bed when we remembered to go upstairs or were left to fall asleep on the sofa or the floor. We were left to sort ourselves out. Often we didn't go to bed until midnight. Sometimes Jayden would take it upon himself to carry us up to bed. I remember waking up in his arms if I fell asleep somewhere in the house. We used to get left on our own a lot because Shane was out all the time and Terri would disappear for periods. We never knew where. Often there were strangers coming in and out of the house. With hindsight, I assume they were drug dealers. It was only years later that I realised what Terri was doing when I used to see her heating tin foil with a lighter.

Terri never stopped drinking. I'd get up in the morning and she would be drunk. Often her best friend, a neighbour, would call round and they drank together. As the day went on they grew louder and louder, and Terri's friend, who also had a young child, then tried to straighten her out before Shane arrived. Ironically, he used her neglect of us as an excuse to beat her. The friend brought toothbrushes and toothpaste round with her to try hide the smell of alcohol on Terri's breath and helped her to dispose of the empty wine and vodka bottles.

I never saw any tenderness or affection between Shane and Terri, just tension and hatred. I don't remember them ever going out or getting a babysitter. They shouted at each other; they didn't talk. There was a fight every day, if not more than once a day. In the end, I learned to block it out and assumed this was normal – I thought it was what people did. I didn't know any other families with young children to make comparisons because we didn't mix. Shane's social life was drinking with his friends and Terri's was drinking at home.

In our own way, we were all affected by the violence. We huddled together and cried, and as we got older we tried to stop Shane, who was often drunk too, but he just swatted us away like flies. The beatings were brutal – he used to smash Terri's head up against the brick arch between the lounge and the kitchen. Drunk and incapable, she took her beatings but sometimes whimpered. Early on she learned not to fight back. She was hospitalised so many times and still the authorities let five children live in the house. They knew what was going on because often the police were called by concerned neighbours.

It was always fists when Shane beat Terri; always sustained and brutal. There was never just a slap. Sometimes I wondered why she never defended herself and hit back. After all, she was tall and big and he was short. I used to think, if she tried, she would have been able to batter him. But fighting back would have made him worse. Obviously very strong, he was also savage.

I should feel sorry for her, and I do understand that she was a victim and suffered terrible abuse, but even in later life when she broke away from Shane, she showed no affection or responsibility for me. She was not a nice person.

One memory stands out from those early years. Later in my life, when counsellors asked about my first memory, it was always the same one that came bubbling to the surface: the image of Terri's bloodied and swollen face being repeatedly forced into the metal sieve of a mop bucket by a snarling Shane, as if he was trying to wring the alcohol out of her.

As he assaulted her, my terrified brothers screamed and ran around him, nappies hanging down around their knees. We all tried to stop him but he was a man possessed.

I don't remember what led to that particular beating, but I assume he came home and she was drunk. The fight took place in the kitchen, where there was an old-fashioned galvanised metal mop and bucket. Shane repeatedly punched Terri until she fell on the floor. Then he grabbed her by the hair, dragged her over to the bucket and shoved her face into the metal grid. I heard bones crunch; it was sickening. He was pushing down on the back of her head so hard that the sinews in his forearms strained. Then he smacked her on the back of the head with the mop.

It was one of the few times she screamed: she was screaming for her life. At one point he knelt on her back and she twisted at such an awkward angle I thought he was going to break her neck. There were trails of blood down the sides of the bucket. Her face became so swollen that when he eventually stopped she was stuck in the bucket. She lay on the floor sobbing and bleeding, with the bucket on her head, twisted like a broken doll.

Terrified and traumatised, my siblings and I cowered in a corner, crying. Shane stood over her, motionless until the sound of police sirens roused him. Whenever the law arrived, he made off like a coward out the back door and down the alleyway at the end of the yard. A neighbour must have called the police.

When they came, Terri had to be cut free from the bucket. Her nose was crooked and pouring blood. She needed to stay in hospital for several days and we were taken into temporary care. Still, we were sent back when she was released. She never filed charges and there were no prosecutions.

I hate Shane for what he did to us and to Terri. But, ironically, later in life he did show some interest in his family. After we were taken into care, he was always the one who turned up on contact visits with sweets and lemonade. He would talk to us and ask about our lives. But from Terri there was nothing: she turned up drunk, looked at her watch repeatedly and asked whether it was time to go as if she couldn't wait to leave. I have never looked up to my birth mother, and I learned from birth never to look to her for anything because there was never anything to look up to.

There was never a time of normality when we lived together as a family. I cannot remember a normal day. I don't recall feeling safe; I didn't know what safety was. If I'd had the choice, back then, I would have liked to live anywhere but that house.

I remember wondering why we were there, and why we'd been born.

In the depths of this miserable home life there was one place where I could be normal and felt secure, if only temporarily. My grandparents' house in the Cheshire countryside was a sanctuary for all of us; an oasis of calm in the midst of the chaos. Terri's adoptive parents, Anne and Malcolm Evans, were the only people we could run away to. In many respects, they were the parents we never had. They looked out for us and knew about some of the problems we faced at home because we sometimes went to stay with them when there was trouble. While our birth parents starved us of affection, they did their best to fill the vacuum. When Terri was hospitalised, or the police were called after a fight, Granddad would make the long journey to take us back to the peace of his home. Like a silver-haired superhero, he swooped in to save the day.

Often the mercy missions would take place in the middle of the night after he had been alerted by a slurred, drunken call from Terri or, if things had got out of hand, a call from the police. Nan and Granddad were the most stable influence in my life at the time. If they weren't rescuing us after one of Shane's onslaughts, they would visit and bring food parcels and clothes. They knew we were never fed or clothed properly and would often arrive with homemade cakes and bags full of groceries, along with warm clothes and essentials like new underwear and pyjamas.

For as long as I can remember, Nan looked like a stereotypical granny. Her grey hair was styled in a tight curly perm. I don't know how old she was when she got it, but I can only ever remember her with that one hairstyle, and I couldn't imagine her as a younger woman. She was tiny, around 5ft 3in, and always seemed to be wearing an apron. Granddad was originally from Manchester and was very tall. He looked like a giant from my vantage point, but he was a friendly one, like something from a children's story.

Nan and Granddad's house was everything ours was not. They were complete opposites. Their house was very homely, it was bright and warm; worlds apart from the dark, dank space we were used to. It had comfortable, soft furnishings; it was clean and it smelled of home cooking. It was also child-friendly. Although we were only there occasionally, they did everything they could to make it welcoming for us. It was a bungalow and, although it was obvious old people lived there because of the old-fashioned furnishings and decor, it still felt like a place where we could be at home. We didn't need to have our guards up when we were there. There were toys for us and beds we could sleep in, with warm duvets and clean sheets. It felt so safe, like no one could get to us when we were there.

Nan would always prepare home-cooked meals when we stayed and, each time we walked in, the smell of roasting meat or home baking filled the house. She used to make banana muffins and we each had our own teacups with little clown faces on them. We usually turned up at the house after a particularly nasty beating, and Nan would sit us down at the table, pour us hot tea and serve up muffins before we collapsed into bed.

Outside there was a lovely garden with a well-kept lawn and colourful borders. Nan and Granddad loved gardening and in warm weather would be outside with us, encouraging us to play and to be the carefree kids we could not be at home. Their bungalow was in a quiet street; our house was on a busy main road and there were always people screaming and shouting outside. Our grandparents' house was quiet and in an area where there were a lot of retired couples. Often the neighbours had their grandchildren over as well and we played with them.

The length of time we stayed there depended on the circumstances at home. If Terri had been hospitalised then we stayed longer, sometimes for up to a week. It was like going on holiday. When it was time to go back, I got anxious. The thought of returning home filled me with uncertainty, and left me torn between two worlds: my home and my grandparents' home. One was warm and cosy, the other was chilly and hostile. Despite realising at a young age that what was happening at home was frightening, I was too young to know how neglected we all were and in my mind the horrific incidents were my normality. To some degree, we all felt a misplaced sense of loyalty towards Shane and Terri, so, when we did get home from our grandparents, we learned to play down the details of the fun we'd had because, if we spoke excitedly about the toys and the games, we were told that we were being spoilt. My little brothers especially didn't want my parents to feel like they were unappreciated.

When we weren't being protected by my grandparents, the job fell to my elder brother, Jayden. He was four years older than me, whereas Kirsten was 11 months older. Jayden took care of us right from the off; he saved our lives on a few occasions. He has always been a big boy and had to grow up rapidly. Even when he was five and six he was making sure we were safe when fights broke out, and by the time he was seven years old, he was standing up to Shane. Jayden wouldn't let him anywhere near us and in the process his protective nature earned him a lot of injuries. On one occasion, he tried to defend Terri by kicking Shane in the privates and then, when our father's anger turned on us, Jayden herded us all into the pantry and locked us in before he ran off to call the police. He learned to dial 999 in an emergency very early on in life.

When I was a little older, I learned that Jayden was not my full brother. Appropriately for Terri and Shane's chaotic, confused life, Jayden's real father was Shane's brother, which makes him my cousin and my brother at the same time. My uncle slept with Terri before she was with Shane but that has never mattered to me and has never altered the way I feel about Jayden. We have had our issues and have fallen out over the years. Jayden has had his demons to face as much as me, thanks to our early years, but I have only ever viewed him as a brother and was always thankful for the way he looked after us. We were always close and in later years, when we were finally taken into care, Jayden was adopted by my nan and granddad and cared for them loyally as they grew older.

Jayden was a gorgeous kid. Always tall for his age, even as a toddler he looked older than his years. He was handsome and had dark hair; always stocky and bulky, but not fat. He was very active and loved sports. They became his escape and I'm sure they were a way he could channel the frustration he felt at home. He played football and especially enjoyed the rough and tumble of rugby. Always fearless, Jayden didn't seem to care about being hurt. Each of us in our own way became immune to pain and fear in our later lives, and we have all had our issues to deal with because of this. We became risk takers and each developed a warped sense of personal safety.

Despite the burden Jayden had to shoulder at home, he was always smiling. He managed to see the best in everyone, or at least he tried to. It was as if he had the maternal instinct Terri should have had. Along with the photographs I have of Terri, I also have pictures of Jayden when he was young, and in them he is often holding me when I was a toddler. He has a defiant look in his eye, like a lioness protecting her young.

When I look at those photographs now they make me feel sad because they remind me of just how quickly we all had to grow up and how much we missed out on. We didn't really have a mother or a father; the adults who were supposed to be protecting and guiding us were not fit for parenthood. We were our own family and, at times, Jayden was our mum and dad. We all looked out for each other and Jayden did his best to keep us safe. In the bitter cold of winter we took care of our younger brothers and made sure they were warm, snuggling up to them and sharing blankets and quilts when the house got so cold you could see your breath in front of your face.

Like a pack of wild animals each of us knew his place in the hierarchy of our dysfunctional family. Jayden was the protector and, along with Kirsten and me, he looked after our two younger brothers when they came along. Jamie arrived first, a year after I was born, and Harry was born a year later.

Kirsten inherited Terri's dark hair, as did Jamie. Her face was thin and she was a scrawny little thing, all bony limbs. In bed, I would often get a spiky elbow or knee in the back whenever she fidgeted around, trying to find a comfortable spot.

Kirsten and I developed a different relationship to the one I had with Jayden. We were so close in age that throughout the years our roles interchanged. When I was young, she acted as the older sister. She taught me the things I should have been taught by adults, such as how to tie a shoelace and how to use cutlery. When we were placed in temporary foster care after fights at home, Kirsten and I would inevitably be put together while the boys were sent elsewhere. It was impossible for social services to find a home where all five of us could be accommodated. In those early years, we were taken away and sent back three times but then there were the times when we were whisked away by my grandparents too.

Social services automatically became involved following any incident the police had attended. Mainly the foster carers looked after us overnight while Terri went off to hospital to be patched up. It was always an adventure when we got back together and we excitedly told each other where we'd been and what we'd been doing. Inevitably, the houses we stayed in were warm and equipped with toys and games for children. As we grew older, the role between Kirsten and me reversed, and she used to get scared and come to me at night for reassurance.

We all learned to hide behind masks. To the outside world, we were gregarious, smiley, friendly children. For my part, I remember being overly eager to please people. Maybe I believed that, if I smiled, I would feel happier and, if I really tried hard to please people, they would give me the love and affection that was so badly lacking from my parents. Kirsten was like me – a smiley and friendly child. She was also very bouncy; she couldn't sit still, bordering on hyperactivity. Whenever she got the freedom of some space, she ran around until she exhausted herself. She craved attention because she didn't get much at home. Extremely excitable, she babbled on for ages whenever anyone engaged her in conversation.

Early on we all started to develop behavioural problems. We were never potty trained by our parents and this affected us. Up until the age of four, I was wearing a nappy. Our levels of personal hygiene were appalling too: we were rarely washed and taught each other how to clean our teeth. Kirsten developed the strange habit of drinking vinegar. If ever there was any in the pantry she would steal it and drink it. If we happened to be out somewhere, and there were sachets of it, she made a beeline for it and filled her pockets. On one occasion after we were taken into care and taken out for a meal, Kirsten disappeared. Eventually she was found under a table in another part of the restaurant, drinking from a bottle of vinegar. On another occasion, she was hospitalised for bingeing on it.

Our lives started to change when my grandparents arranged for us all to go to a nearby nursery. It was the first time we had been given any structure. Most likely they realised our lives were in freefall and wanted to help us get some form of normality. Perhaps they realised that the longer we were able to escape from the misery of our house, the healthier we would be.

Going to nursery was like stepping foot on another planet. The rooms were brightly painted, warm and full of toys; the staff there were welcoming and engaging. They loved children and enjoyed being around them – they cared. At home we were left to our own devices, but in nursery our days were structured and we had activities to occupy us. The environment was safe, no one was shouted at and we were given hot meals.

I can only imagine the condition we were in when we arrived. Our clothes would have been dirty and smelly and, on several occasions, we were sent home with clothes from the lost property box because they were a better alternative to what we were wearing. We scoffed whatever food was put in front of us. When I was much older, I also learned from social services documents that I was suffering from scabies, an infectious skin condition caused by mites that burrow into the skin. This, coupled with the asthma and eczema I suffered, would have made me a poorly sight. It was at the nursery that people began to notice we were being neglected because my files show that it was around this time that the social services department in the area we lived began to take an active interest in me. It must have been obvious just looking at all of us, and observing the way we behaved, that things at home were not right. I was only three or four when I started going there; I hadn't socialised with other kids, I didn't know how to communicate properly or have a conversation with anyone who wasn't a sibling. At first I couldn't speak to an adult without looking at the floor but the staff there were so nice and friendly, they encouraged me and I looked up to them – it was like going on holiday each time I went there.

I was so overwhelmed by the caring nature of the people at the nursery that it gave me the lifelong ambition to work in a care environment. In those early years the only meaningful interaction I had with adults other than my grandparents was with police officers, ambulance drivers who came to take Terri away and nursery staff. Ever since then all I have wanted to do is to work as a police officer, a paramedic or in the care industry. I've always wanted to protect or help people.

The nursery also opened me up to the world of words and numbers and stories. At home, we were never read to and we didn't have books. Through nursery, we began to learn the alphabet and to string letters together to form simple words. Back at home, Kirsten and I would spend a lot of the time helping each other to learn things, remembering what we had been taught at nursery that day. Terri and Shane never took an interest in what we were doing or whether we were learning anything. As I grew older, I remember Terri was becoming more engrossed in drug taking. I didn't know what was happening at the time but I do remember how she would hold a lighter under a spoon and chase the fumes with a straw, and I can only imagine with us at nursery her drug taking and drinking grew worse as she had more time to indulge herself.

She was often frazzled when she came and picked us up and took us home, when she spent ages trying to hide the bottles she had drunk that day (she never bothered with glasses, wine and spirits were slugged straight from the bottle). She was almost childlike in the haphazard way she tried to cover her tracks. She folded pieces of paper around bottles in the hope that Shane would ignore them. It was surreal; she had a complete lack of sense. I remember her with a bottle in one hand and a fag in the other, dropping ash on the floor; being a mess and tripping up around the house, but never passing out.

Terri never did anything with us. She never sat down with Kirsten and me to do our hair or play with us. The truth was, she didn't care and the older I got, the less I cared about her. I hated her for being with Shane, and I hated him for attacking her.

It's hard to feel sad about the situation because there was never affection, so there was never any loss to mourn.

Chapter three

MOVING ON

Often there were strange men in the house. I assume now that they must have been drug pushers, supplying Terri. Mainly, people stayed away – it wasn't the kind of place you'd want to visit or would feel comfortable in. One of the few visitors who did come on a fairly regular basis was a distant relative called Pat. I wasn't sure who he was related to but I dreaded him coming. He would often arrive with Shane after the two of them had been drinking. They would come barging through the door, carrying cans of Skol, and drunkenly terrorise us all for the rest of the night. After turning on loud music, they would order Terri around, directing her to get them food and more alcohol. Sometimes she was hit if she didn't do as they said; often she joined in the party.

Pat was a large, sweaty man with a foul mouth – he didn't care whether there were children in the room or not. He would cuss and shout and, depending on his mood, became aggressive. Around 5ft 10in tall, he had a large, protruding belly; often it poked out from the bottom of the T-shirts and vests he wore. I only ever saw him in polyester tracksuit bottoms and he stank of beer, bad breath and body odour. Bald, with tattoos on both his arms, he was never smart or washed. His teeth looked like yellow tombstones; crooked and rotten in bloodied gums.

I was terrified of him and whenever I heard him come into the house I would hide under the dirty blanket that was sometimes left on the couch by whoever had slept on it the previous night. Praying he wouldn't see me, I would close my eyes and try to cover myself completely, sinking between the cushions. But Pat would always come and find me and, whenever he did, he touched me.

It started when I was around three. Thankfully, I only remember fragments of what occurred. I don't know where my parents were when it happened and I don't remember my brothers or sister being there with me; I know that often I found myself alone with him. Fixing me with a faraway look, his eyes would become hooded and dark.

'Come here,' he growled. 'All kids do it. Your dad says it's allowed.'

I didn't know whether this was true or not, but he was an adult and as a child I believed everything adults said.

His breath stank as he leaned towards me. I was so confused, I couldn't understand what he was doing or why he was doing it, but I knew it made me feel uncomfortable. I tried to squirm out of his grasp but he just laughed and pawed at me with his dirty, rough hands. Sometimes I heard Shane laughing drunkenly somewhere else in the house or Terri shouting. Often I could hear the footsteps of my brothers and sister on the floorboards upstairs and wished for Jayden to come in and save me. I wanted to be invisible; to fall asleep and wake up when it was all over.

There were times when I tried to tell Terri what was happening to me. I didn't have the words to describe the act and instead I told her that I was hurting. Either she couldn't understand what I was trying to say because her brain was so addled with booze or she didn't want to understand and address the situation. She just looked at me mutely or told me I would feel better after a little while.

As I grew older, the abuse became more frequent. I told myself this was normal; it was how adults behaved towards children. I had been let down and beaten by adults all my life, I didn't expect anything else from them.

As I got bigger, Shane's aggression towards me and the rest of the family escalated. I still have the scars to remind me.

By the age of four I was developing enough courage to tell him when I thought he had been particularly cruel. This streak of defiance, he told me, was down to my 'fiery tongue'. One day, in a drunken haze, he decided to try to cut it off.

He pinned both my arms down and waved a knife in front of my eyes. I struggled and wept but that only seemed to encourage him.

'I'm going to sharpen my knife on that fiery tongue of yours,' he slurred.

He began to scrape the knife around my mouth and chin. 'Show me that tongue,' he persisted.

Determined not to let him have his way I kept my mouth clamped firmly shut. Inside, I was terrified.

Then I felt a searing pain under my chin. He had pushed the knife in hard enough to puncture my skin. Feeling the blood trickle down my neck, I whimpered. I couldn't understand why any adult would treat a child in this way, let alone a father and his own daughter. He got off me and tried to stop the bleeding but I needed to go to hospital to have the wound glued shut. I'm not sure what excuse he gave them, but obviously he didn't tell them the truth because there were no repercussions.

I also remember being hospitalised for another knife incident when my finger was slashed open, but thankfully the full memory of that particular episode has been buried in my mind.

Shane was crazy. I've no doubt if anyone knew the full extent of his behaviour he would have been sectioned and locked away. A danger to the public and a danger to his own family, he lived and breathed violence. It wasn't just Terri and his kids he attacked, he got in fights all the time. I once heard him boast about smashing in someone's face in the pub and breaking someone else's nose; I remember times when he came home with blood on his clothes, bruises and swelling on his face, and scraped knuckles. He was excitable and drunk, and talked about how hard he was to scare us; he made sure we all knew the levels of violence he was capable of. Violence had been a theme throughout his life. The last time I heard about him, much later on in my adult life, was through the newspaper report about his attack on the two women.

The piece mentioned that he had scores of convictions. As children, we didn't need to be told how hard he was because we already knew: it was evident to us how aggressive he was because of the beatings dished out to Terri. Then, when we were older, he told us his fighting tales in the way that old soldiers tell their war stories.

Despite his fearsome reputation, he made more and more of an effort to stay out of Jayden's way. I'm not sure why – Jayden was still only a child. He grew up into a strapping man you wouldn't want to mess with, but as a child Shane could easily have coped with him. I can only think his reluctance to cross swords was because Jayden was his brother's son and perhaps his brother was also a violent man and, had he found out that Shane was beating Jayden, he would have avenged his son.

We never had days out with our parents; we were never taken places and treated. The nearest we ever got to having a day out was when the police came and took us away. We spent a lot of time at the police station and it was a treat to go there: we loved the excitement of being taken to a new place where there were people who talked to us, entertained us and gave us food and drink. The police officers who looked after us were always lovely. They knew how tough we were having it at home, having noted the state we were in when we were taken in. We all wore a mish-mash of clothing picked from whatever was lying around on the floor at the time. There was no organisation in the house and no one ever bothered to make sure we were suitably dressed so, more often than not, we wore odd shoes and odd socks – we just grabbed whatever fitted. The police officers noticed this and often raided the lost property department for clothes for us. They always managed to find toys for us to play with and spent time talking to us; they even allowed us to wear their hats. It was a real adventure going to the police station and we became regular visitors.

I would have happily lived in the local station; I wanted to stay there forever. The policemen were especially protective. Knowing what I know now, it must have been hard for them to see the state of neglect we were in and still have to hand us back to our parents because Terri never pressed charges against Shane. The officers often said they were going to stop him doing it again each time an attack happened, and, although I wanted to believe them, I always knew in the back of my mind that once I was home there was nothing they could do. However, they were very kind and I've no doubt they did the best they could in a system in which their hands were largely tied. In those days, domestic incidents were not treated with the same severity as they are today. At least they tried to return us home clean, well fed and clothed. On one occasion, my sister and I were playing in a room at the station when one of the male officers noticed we were wearing dirty, scuffed, odd shoes.

'Your shoes don't match,' he frowned.

'They never do,' shrugged Kirsten.

'Come with me,' he said.

We were taken out of the station and down the local high street, where the kindly officer found a shoe shop and took us in to be measured. He bought us both a new pair of trainers.

Mine had flashing lights in the soles, which lit up whenever I started running. They reminded me of the police cars that would arrive after a fight to take us off to safety.

I didn't know it at the time but things were changing. The attacks and incidents were being noted. Our lives were being monitored, and Shane and Terri were running out of chances. The police had been called too often; the nursery had reported too many incidents of neglect.

The final incident, which set my siblings and me on a new course in life, happened one night when I was around four or five. Shane had been out all night; we hadn't seen him so it had been a relatively quiet evening. The only drama we had to contend with was Terri's drunkenness, which we were so used to by this stage that it would have been strange if she was sober. She had fallen asleep somewhere but Jayden had checked on her to make sure she was still breathing and wasn't choking on vomit or unconscious. We all started going to bed, or falling asleep in dribs and drabs.

At some point, in the early hours of the morning, Shane stumbled in, drunk. Again, this was nothing new, and I had learned to sleep through the noise. However, on this occasion he came into the bedroom and started to shuffle around in the dark. This was something that never happened and so I started to wake.

The next thing I heard as the fog of sleep cleared from my head was a roar from Shane and a scream. Initially I was confused, Shane was shouting and I heard one of my brothers howl in pain. He sounded terrified.

The light went on and I saw Harry, who was only a toddler, screaming and holding the back of his head. There was blood seeping through his fingers. Next to him, on the dirty bed sheets, was a kitchen knife. Shane, suddenly sober, was staring at him in horror. It was the first time I had ever seen him scared.

'It was supposed to be your mother,' he stuttered.

Pandemonium broke out as each of us children began screaming. This scared Harry even more. Jayden, who had been asleep somewhere else in the house, burst in.

'What have you done?' he screamed, scanning the scene in front of him.

Shane looked at him, turned and ran.

The ambulance and police arrived within minutes. Jayden called them. The house was filled with flashing blue lights as medics and police officers hurried around the house. Terri was somewhere in the middle of the chaos, confused about what was going on. I didn't see her.

Whatever tensions were apparent between her and Shane that day must have been building up to the point where he decided he wanted to kill her. And so after a long boozing session he returned home, grabbed a knife and went straight to the room where he thought she was and stabbed out in the dark. In the event, among the pile of bodies in the bed, he hit Harry instead. He got him in the back of the skull. There was a lot of blood but luckily the blade did not penetrate bone and, although Harry needed several stitches, he was not seriously hurt. He was taken off in an ambulance to be stitched up and, as the shock subsided, it became an adventure for him. He'd already seen so much violence in his short life, he was used to it.

I learned later that Shane was arrested nearby. After questioning we were taken from our home to the police station and, a short while later, someone from the local social services came to speak to us. They explained that we would be sent to stay with temporary foster carers that night. It was doubtful we would all be able to go to the same house, so Kirsten and I would be sent somewhere and the boys would be sent somewhere else.

Wherever it was we ended up that evening we were exhausted. The following weeks were a merry-go-round of different placements. Often people from social services arrived and talked to us. We stayed with different people in around five or six houses. The movements seemed to take place on a weekly basis. I wasn't aware of the process at the time, but we were being shuttled between foster carers while a more permanent home was found for us. We had been placed in temporary care before so we knew the drill. In each home, there would be clothes and food provided; we didn't have our own possessions. Normally the people we stayed with were well meaning and tried to engage with us and keep us occupied. Sometimes we stayed in big houses with gardens and had our own rooms, but Kirsten would inevitably sneak into my room at night and come into bed with me. We had been so used to sharing a bed she was scared and exposed on her own. Sometimes we would be placed in a flat and shared a room. The people we stayed with were always couples or single women. We didn't get attached because we always knew we were moving on.

We didn't really understand the implications of what was happening. We weren't told what had happened to Shane and Terri, but I didn't care. I didn't know that Shane had been charged over the stabbing or that Terri was in rehab.

We tumbled through the care system until we were told by social workers that we were going to live with a nice couple in a town several miles away. They were called Graham and Pauline and they had an older son, who was adopted. We weren't given any choice in the matter and, again, I didn't care. Although I didn't understand it at the time, I didn't miss anything about our house and I didn't miss anything about my parents. The people I really missed were my brothers. At various times, we were brought together for visits, usually in places like play or leisure centres. During those visits, we hugged and excitedly told each other where we had been and what we had been doing. And always we played because we had the luxury and freedom of being able to be children. Harry proudly showed off his stitches, prominent on the patch of scalp that had to be shaved so the medics could clean and care for his wound.

I was always sad when it was time to leave but the social workers who facilitated the meetings assured us that we would see each other again.

Eventually Shane was sent to jail and Terri remained in rehab. Our dysfunctional family was finished and the police had finally delivered on their promise: Shane was locked up and couldn't hurt us anymore. The scars from those early years, however, were deep-set and had an effect on all of us. For my part, I was having behavioural issues. Kirsten and I were mixed up. We had trouble accepting adult authority and bonding with anyone or trusting them. And we had been split up from our brothers, which was deeply upsetting and unsettling. We had formed such a tight unit to survive that to suddenly be apart felt isolating and far more scary than anything we'd had to deal with in the previous years.

The plans were finalised after about six weeks of being moved around. Harry and Jamie were to be adopted by a couple who lived several miles away. They had a new home and a new life. Jayden was to be adopted by Nan and Granddad. I later learned that they had wanted to keep us all and, if we had the choice, that was where we would have wanted to be. However, as Nan and Granddad were old, social services deemed that they would not be capable of providing the sort of environment we needed. Instead, they agreed to let them have Jayden because he was the eldest. He moved to Cheshire to be with them.

Kirsten and I were placed with the couple we had been told about on a long-term temporary basis while the authorities tried to find someone who would take us on permanently. Partly I was excited by the movement and not knowing where we would end up. I had never experienced certainty or security; I was used to living from day to day, not knowing what would happen or where I would end up – whether that was the hospital or the police station.

In those weeks after the knife attack, I never thought about my parents. I didn't care what happened to them. When I was told by a social worker that Shane had been jailed, I was glad. I knew my life was better without him in it and both he and Terri had failed me so often, I didn't grieve for them, miss them or even worry about what was happening to them as I was becoming immune to the emotions I should have been feeling in such uncertain circumstances. Stuff just happened and I moved on.

We never went back to the house and we never lived together again as siblings, which was sad as we had formed such a special bond under the extreme circumstance. We also never lived with our parents again, and while I missed my brothers and sister, quite simply, I did not care if I ever saw Terri or Shane again.

Chapter four

FOREVER FAMILIES

Graham and Pauline had a very nice house in the suburbs of a town an hour's drive away from where I had lived previously. Kirsten and I didn't know how long we were going to be living with them. In social services speak we were told the stay would be long term but not permanent. We started to hear the language and phrases that you come across in the care system. Graham and Pauline were not a 'forever family', they were the stepping-stone until we found someone who would permanently adopt us. They were older than the other people we had been placed with, which is quite possibly why they were not considered suitable to have us forever. I think they must have been in their fifties and, in comparison to where we had come from, they were settled and stable with a good home.

Pauline was a kind lady with good intentions. However, Graham made me feel uncomfortable. Sometimes he would walk around the house naked, which I found creepy. He was an old man and it turned my stomach. I was beginning to realise that the care system was a hotchpotch of characters; some were good-natured and kind, others were evil and many more were just plain weird. Most seemed to have as many issues as the kids they were supposed to be looking after.

Graham and Pauline's house was big, smart and very well kept. I can only imagine the expressions on their faces when Kirsten and I arrived. We looked like a couple of orphans – grubby, badly behaved and dressed in mismatched clothes. Then again, we came from a stinking hellhole. Their house resembled a show home. We had no manners, no table manners and hygiene issues. Practically feral, we had never been encouraged to clean or look after ourselves. It was a complete culture shock to go from where we had lived to such an ordered, pristine environment and I hated it.

Pauline and Graham were fanatical about their garden, which was manicured and stocked to bursting with pretty shrubs and flowers. It was their pride and joy. Their love of gardening bordered on the obsessive; it looked like they lived in a garden centre. Pauline especially would spend hours and hours outside whenever the weather allowed. Never happier than when she was up to her elbows in mud, kneeling on the lawn to tend her borders, she encouraged Kirsten and me to take an interest in the garden and we loved having the space to run around. She explained what all the different plants were and what had to be done to care for them. In summer, she would take us into the garden and pick flowers with us and, in the autumn, we would pick fruit from the trees. She would make delicious apple pies and poached pears.

The detached house was posh and spotless but it was too clean. It was so perfect I was scared to do anything that would mess it up. The lovely plush sofas in the lounge had plastic covers on them so they didn't get dirty. It puzzled me why someone would invite children into their house and then not make it child-friendly. Although Pauline did nice things with us and spent time with us, she was adamant that we kept the house pristine. She encouraged us to spend as much time as possible in the garden but then told us off if we stepped mud into the house. It didn't seem fair but, if we tried to explain that to her, we got told off for being cocky.

She also took an interest in what we wore. We arrived with no clothes and had been used to wearing whatever was provided for us in the homes we stayed in. Pauline bought us completely new wardrobes... and all the outfits were the same. She dressed us like twins and, possibly because she was older, she chose old-fashioned clothes. Previously we'd been decked out in trackie bottoms and hoodies but Pauline insisted we wore little dresses, most of them frilly with floral prints. We looked like extras from that TV show *Little House on the Prairie*. I just didn't feel like me – it felt like someone else was trying to force their personality on me.

Worse still, we were made to go to church and Sunday school. We were sent off with friends of theirs (they didn't go). Each Sunday we were dressed in our pretty, twee little dresses and packed off to the local church, where we sang hymns and prayed, and then afterwards we were herded into the church hall next door to learn about Jesus and colour in pictures of bible stories. I had never been to church before and I hadn't even been christened. Soon I was utterly bored by the whole thing and, within a couple of weeks, I started to misbehave and run away. Looking back, I think Pauline and Graham were probably on some sort of misguided mission to save our souls and educate us.

There were strict boundaries laid down at their house. We were told what was expected of us. But we had never had boundaries before and we didn't know how we were supposed to respond to them. We were expected to help with the cleaning and to keep a normal routine, which meant chores and a set bedtime. So we helped out, we did the dishes, and I realise now that it was really good as we needed the discipline but underneath it all there seemed to be this weird undercurrent. I think they believed they had a duty to make us little angels; they were on a crusade to exorcise the evil of our past and, to some degree, it was almost scarier than where we had been previously, because at least there I knew who the enemy was.

As the months progressed, I bonded with Pauline. She took me for days out and she gave us attention. She spent time with both of us and did cooking. I didn't bond with Graham at all, though – he gave me the creeps.

Although we were like savages when we arrived, I picked things up quickly and Pauline did understand about our behavioural problems (she had been briefed by social services). She had patience and we were never told off for not having table manners because she understood it was not our fault. When we were behaving, we were always very polite but, every now and then, we would do something that would cause concern.

One morning I was in the bathroom and I saw Graham's razor on the shelf. I'd seen adverts of men shaving and so I thought I'd try it to see what it felt like. It didn't occur to me that women and children didn't shave. No one had explained about shaving so I reached up and got the razor. I didn't understand that you needed shaving foam so I just copied what I'd seen on the Gillette adverts on TV, drawing the razor up and down my face. It felt smooth but caught on my skin every few centimetres. As well as vertical strokes, I also pulled the razor horizontally across my skin – I assumed the red lines it left were normal. After a few minutes, my face was a smear of blood and I realised something was wrong. I ran out of the bathroom to show Kirsten. She took one look at the blood dripping from my cheeks and neck and screamed.

'Lauren's dying!' she cried.

Pauline came running up the stairs and her eyes widened when she saw me. Her reaction scared me and I started crying.

'Oh, God, what have you done to yourself?' she exclaimed.

'I was shaving,' I sobbed.

She took me in the bathroom and tried to clean me up but the bleeding wouldn't stop, so she drove me to hospital. Although there was a lot of blood, the cuts were not deep so there wasn't much they could do apart from apply ointment to make sure there was no infection and put plasters on the bigger cuts.

Pauline sometimes got stressed by situations but usually took incidents such as this in her stride. To me she seemed like Hyacinth Bucket in the comedy series *Keeping Up Appearances*. She spoke in a posh accent and she was slightly eccentric too. She would talk to a huge teddy bear that she kept in the lounge. I was terrified of it – I was convinced it would tell her if I was naughty.

Although the house never felt like a home, I do have some good memories of it. For the first time in our lives, we went on holidays. We were taken on a boat trip, a big cruise ship, to the Isle of Man. We also went to Butlins, and Nan and Granddad came to visit us there. In the evenings, we all settled in the lounge and watched old people's telly, like *Last of the Summer Wine*.

Christmas was a spectacular affair with Pauline and Graham: they went over the top with decorations and competed with the neighbours to create the most festive themed house. They strung hundreds of lights over the front of the building and the front garden. Graham spent a whole day preparing the display, which must have cost hundreds. There were novelty decorations such as Santas and snowmen dotted around the front garden, which was transformed into a grotto from the start of December until after New Year. We were led outside once everything was in place and then the switch was flicked, which lit up the whole house. People used to visit just to see the lights.

Christmas Day was all about food. We got presents but we were not spoilt. Pauline cooked traditional Christmas lunch with all the trimmings and started preparing weeks before the day. She made fabulous Christmas cakes. My favourites were her homemade coconut-covered teacakes.

While living there, Kirsten and I started a new primary school and I settled into the routine easily – I was always very optimistic about meeting people and confident when it came to making friends; however, I was emotionally unstable. I had difficulty moderating my moods. Often I didn't know how I felt; I would smile one minute and cry the next. I was confused. Sometimes I didn't know who I was or how I was supposed to act.

In all, I was with Pauline and Graham for two years, which was an unusually long time to be in foster care. There were some good times but there were difficult bits too. I never warmed to Graham and some of his habits unsettled me. He was too open when it came to nudity and I found this worrying, especially after the abuse I had suffered at the hands of Pat.

All the while, the plan was to find Kirsten and me a permanent family to live with but, because we were to be adopted together, there were fewer candidates willing to take us on. Our reports, which prospective parents were given, also detailed the neglect and abuse we had suffered with our parents and most likely would have put many potential adopters off. None of them would have been given the details of my history of sexual abuse because, although I had explained what had happened to the social workers, I was never taken seriously. Nothing was ever investigated.

This meant that whoever did eventually become my forever family would not know the full facts of what they were getting themselves into.

Amazingly, in the background while all this was going on, Terri and Shane still had a say in where we went. They were more than happy to be rid of us but were required to approve whatever placements we had. Terri agreed to every single foster placement I had been on. Shane didn't, and just wanted to attack everyone; he didn't want us to be in care. Although he himself wouldn't have taken us on, he didn't want anyone else to have us – he was that sort of person. Neither of them ever showed any guilt over the way they treated us.

Throughout our time with Pauline and Graham we attended parties organised by social services for children in care. People wishing to adopt came along too. The events were billed as parties but, really, they were shop windows for potential adoptive parents to view the kids the council had on its books. We all wore nametags, so if someone liked us they knew who we were. The mayor always attended and gave out awards to children – I'm not sure what the criteria was for winning but I never got one. I used to enjoy these events because there would be plenty of party food and I got the chance to see my brothers there.

As the years passed I began to realise that I was different. As a child in care you are treated differently, when really all you want is to be treated the same as everyone else. Teachers were overly sensitive, which at times bordered on pity. I had friends who had stable families and they never said anything or made me feel differently, but there were rules about the way I could live, which didn't apply to them. For example, I had a best friend called Samantha at school, but I could never go round her house because I was in care. I wasn't allowed on sleepovers unless the parents of the person I was staying with had been approved by the council and passed security checks. And I wasn't allowed on school trips without special permission from my case worker. I was in the care system and, because of that, I was classed as vulnerable, even though I was living long term with Pauline and Graham.

Just after the second anniversary of our placement, Kirsten and I received a visit from one of the social workers who had been involved in our case. There had always been regular contact with social workers and in lieu of not having parents who were capable of looking after us we had someone assigned to us called a 'guardian ad litem'. This was a person appointed by the court for any child who was subject to court proceedings. Usually they were social workers who had a judicial role; we rarely saw ours. Instead, we saw social workers like the one who came that day. She saw us often and had been speaking about a possible forever family in a nearby town. She had mentioned a name, Barbara, and seemed very keen that the placement should work out.

'She is a very caring lady. She has two teenage children and a partner who is lovely but who doesn't live with her,' she explained. 'She is very keen to meet you.'

But I was indifferent about the whole thing. I'd been told that Pauline and Graham were not going to be permanent carers so I was always waiting to be moved on. In some respects, I was glad the time was finally arriving.

On the visit in question the social worker seemed anxious. She had some news to share before she spoke further about how our planned adoption was progressing.

'It's my duty to tell you that your father has been sentenced to time in prison,' she said quietly. Despite the fact that Shane and Terri were not our legal guardians anymore, the social workers had a duty to tell us whenever anything happened to one of them that would affect the infrequent visits we had with them. Often we heard that Terri was in hospital for one thing or another, but this time the news was that once again Shane had been jailed. I'm not sure of the full details but, as most of his convictions were for violence, I assumed he had beaten someone up.

It didn't bother me to hear that we wouldn't be seeing him for a while but Kirsten took the news badly and started crying. The social worker tried to cheer her up.

'But I have good news too,' she said, ushering us to the sofa. 'Sit down and turn on the TV, I have something to show you.'

Pauline and Graham must have known about the surprise as they stood in the background, smiling as she pulled a DVD from her bag and put it in the DVD player.

The screen lit up to show a woman's grinning face.

'Hiya, I wanna be your new mum,' she said softly. She was wearing a bright-green top and her dyed blonde hair was scraped back off her face.

I laughed – I didn't know what else to do. The woman on the screen looked funny; her outfit made her look like Kermit the Frog. Kirsten was silent.

'This is Barbara,' explained the social worker as the woman on the screen babbled on about how excited she was to meet us. 'She has a lovely home, which she wants to share with you. How do you feel about that, Lauren?'

'I'm hungry,' I replied.

I got up and walked into the kitchen to see if there was any cake. When I came back out, it was explained to me that Barbara was what is called a 'prospective adoptive parent' and that she would be coming to visit us with her teenage children to see if we all got along. The social worker kept repeating what a nice lady she was and how much she loved kids.

'It will mean that you girls can both stay together, which is very important,' she said.

It had been over two years since we were taken into care and Barbara was the first adoptive parent we had heard about. I imagine that the people in charge of adoptions were very keen for things to work out between Barbara and us. It certainly seemed that way.

In the following weeks, we had three introductory meetings. Barbara and her family came to visit us at Pauline and Graham's on a Sunday afternoon. It all felt very awkward. She arrived with her two children: David, 12, and Sharon, 15. When she first saw us she beamed and looked us up and down like someone might eye a new dress on a hanger.

'Aren't you gorgeous?' she said.

Pauline and Graham had dressed us in matching dresses and put our hair in bunches.

It was immediately apparent that Barbara and Pauline were complete opposites. Barbara had a gruff, loud voice and spoke with a different accent. She wore clothes that looked far too young for her. She wore skintight jeans and a tight top with a plunging neck; her ample cleavage was pouring out the top. Her hair was highlighted in different shades of blonde. She was what you might describe as rough and ready, with hard features and a nose ring. Although she was in her late thirties, she looked a lot older. She was a smoker and she didn't work.

She brought along her partner, Paul. He was quiet. They had been together for a long time but did not live together and were not adopting as a couple. Her children seemed fun, too, and, while she spoke with Pauline and Graham, we all played wheelbarrows in the garden together. As they were older than we were, we thought they were cool.

We didn't speak about very much on the first meeting. Barbara asked general questions – what school did we go to? What were our favourite lessons? What television shows did we like? She seemed excited but I wasn't. With hindsight, I know now that we were being processed through a system. Barbara was to have three meetings with us, all observed by a social worker, and she would have fulfilled a set criterion before she was allowed to take us home. It was a formal procedure designed to get children out of care and into permanent homes, where the council no longer had a financial obligation to look after them. Foster carers were paid money; adoptive parents were not.

After that first meeting, we met Barbara twice more. I wasn't particularly interested and at one meeting recall sitting outside with my portable CD player listening to music through headphones. I knew we were moving on, and I didn't want to stay with Pauline and Graham. Already I had detached myself from the situation. Although we had some nice times, I had never allowed myself to become attached to them because I knew it was not going to be forever.

After the meetings, Kirsten and I never spoke about them or what was going to happen. We never discussed moving to a new family. At that time, I don't think either of us understood what family meant. We stayed with people, they bought us clothes and fed us but we had never experienced family. We didn't know how to behave and this lack of structure was becoming increasingly obvious the older we got. We were so independent, we were at times uncontrollable. Kirsten was especially wild: if she didn't want to do something she wouldn't. She didn't want to get to know people, and she didn't want to bond. We had no reason to believe that a move to Barbara's or anywhere else would be permanent; we had no concept of what permanent meant. Kirsten was eight and she didn't trust anyone; I was a year younger and I didn't know how I was supposed to act around adults. Half the time I would do everything I could to please them and make them like me; other times they would make me angry and I would misbehave and test them.

After the meetings with Barbara the social worker visited again. She was very excited.

'Do you like her?' she asked.

I shrugged.

'Well, she loves you, she can't wait for you to go and live with her.'

And that was that. We were going to a new town with a new family – a forever family. There were three weeks to prepare.

Once again our lives were about to change.

Chapter five

ALONE

During our time with Pauline and Graham, we had contact visits with Shane and Terri, although we never saw them together. After the stabbing incident, in 1996, they split up. Each visit was attended by all my siblings and their social workers. Because we were such a big family, and each set of children had their own case worker and guardians, there would be a crowd of us. The meetings were supervised; the social workers were there to observe and report. A few were in the Wacky Warehouse play centre, where we would go off and play, while Terri would sit in the corner, bored. The idea of the visits was to maintain some sort of a family structure and allow us all to keep in contact. By that time we were being offered for adoption so there was never any suggestion that at some point we would go back to live with Terri if she sorted herself out.

While Terri would be indifferent, Shane would make an effort to show an interest. He would ask what we had been doing and if we had been good, and he used to goad the social workers. We knew we were never going back and that took Shane's power away. I despise both my birth parents but on those visits I think Shane did at least try to make some kind of effort. I don't think he ever felt bad about what he'd done, or guilty about the way he treated us, because he wasn't a remorseful person but I think he felt bad about the situation. When he saw how happy we were when we were all together, I'm sure he felt bad that we had been split up largely due to his actions.

I loved seeing my brothers. As soon as we saw each other, it was as if we had never been apart. It was a struggle being away from them after all we had been through, and the visits allowed us to be a family again. We would run around and wear ourselves out and forget that anyone else was there. It was just us; it really didn't matter if Terri or Shane were present or not, we weren't interested. When Terri wandered off for a cigarette none of us wondered where she'd gone; we were with each other and that was all that mattered.

Each of us was affected by what had happened. Kirsten was becoming increasingly unruly. I was overly affectionate. Jamie was shy and timid – all he wanted to do was hug me and sit on my lap. Sometimes we played Barbie dolls together. We used to talk a lot while the others were off doing things; he was very calm while everyone else was hyperactive. He used to like doing my hair – I had really long hair and he would tie it up for me. Harry was the opposite. He was a little rascal; he would run around bossing everyone. Jayden was quiet and brooding.

The visits happened between three and four times a year and we also saw Nan and Granddad once a year. But it was not enough: we had all shared difficult times and survived them together and to go from living closely every day to hardly seeing each other was hard to adjust to.

Visits would end with us being separated. It was awful when we were taken away. We didn't care about leaving Terri or Shane, but it was heartbreaking to leave each other. We literally had to be dragged off each other and we were all crying. Jayden tried to calm us down and assure us that we would see each other again but we all knew it wouldn't be for many months. Jamie and I clung onto each other or ran away and hid. Sometimes we needed to be restrained, screaming and kicking. It felt as if we lived a million miles apart: even though we were all still quite close geographically, it was obvious our lives were moving in different directions. We could have seen each other more, but the authorities deemed there was to be no contact in between the arranged visits, which were closely supervised and two hours in duration.

We were rationed.

I later realised that locations had been chosen that did not have clocks in them so we were unaware when the visits were going to end, so we couldn't run away together. However, I learned to recognise the looks on the adults' faces. They became increasingly anxious when each visit was up because they knew they would have to tell us it was time to go.

When I think about those visits now, I can only conclude that the system majorly failed us all. It was awful: we went from a family unit, which was dysfunctional but close-knit, to seeing each other three times a year. It was like being torn away from familiarity. I often felt isolated and it was so cruel, having that irregular contact. We never knew when it was going to be so we didn't have it to look forward to, and when it happened it was for two hours, which goes so fast when you are having fun. We never saw each other without Terri or Shane in the background, which was a distraction. It was almost as if the system was designed to break the sibling bond down, rather than maintain it, which is what eventually started to happen.

Thanks to those visits, I can now instantly recognise children on contacts. And at the time it was very clear to other people that we were on a contact and in care. The signs were easy to spot; we were accompanied by people who looked businesslike and authoritative. No matter how much the social workers tried to blend in, it was easy to tell. While Shane and the other parents wore tracksuits, they would wear formal clothes and carry briefcases and notepads. There were five of us who looked similar but we all arrived at different times, with different adults. The first thing we did was hug and kiss. It would have been better if we had been allowed to meet in the car park, getting the initial greetings out of the way so we could then walk in together. People would look at us with a mixture of pity and embarrassment as the story unfolded before them.

Once it had been decided that we were going to live with Barbara we were swiftly moved on. We were enrolled in a new school in the new town where we were going to live, and our new uniforms were bought for us. We hardly had anything to pack. As Pauline and Graham were fosterers, the clothes and toys we had stayed with them, ready for the next children to arrive at their door. We only had a small bag each with a few toys and a few clothes to tide us over. Barbara had bought us both a new wardrobe. I felt like a doll, being passed between people and dressed according to their taste.

Barbara, her partner Paul and her children came to pick us up. Pauline saw us off and stood crying in the front doorway as we climbed into Barbara's car. Graham stood next to her, impassive. I wouldn't hug them before I left – I didn't want to. It was awkward, it always was when the time came to say goodbye. We had lived there for two years and then overnight we were off, never to meet again. It was the same in all the placements we had; a line was drawn underneath them. I was used to that but it still felt weird; I became adept at forgetting and putting emotions aside.

The journey to our new home was fun. We stopped on the way for a McDonald's, and Barbara's children, David and Sharon, were friendly and seemed genuinely excited about having new people in the house. They had bought us each a keychain with the letters L and K on them.

The house was in a rough part of town. When we pulled up outside it reminded me of the street we lived in with Terri and Shane. The houses were unkempt and they all looked the same. Barbara's house was featureless from the front, just like the others. Inside you walked down a dark hallway, which had a bedroom leading off it and opened up into the living room, which was lime green and almost the same shade as the top Barbara had worn in her introductory DVD. The whole house was badly decorated – the wallpapering wasn't finished and the kitchen was very small.

It was a four-bedroom property. Kirsten and I shared a room, which suited us as, despite the fact that Barbara was now our prospective mother-to-be, she was still a stranger and the house was a strange environment. Having seen little in our short lives to convince us that adults could be trusted, we felt safer together in the same room. We had bunk beds and, for a long time after we moved in, Kirsten, who slept on the bottom, still preferred to sleep in the same bed and climbed up the back of the bed when the lights went out to get under the covers with me. It was a scruffy house and, with four children, it felt cramped. It was very different to Pauline and Graham's much bigger house.

When we arrived, Barbara had done all our clothes shopping for us. We didn't have a say in how we were to be dressed and she had decided to put us in identical outfits, as if we were twins, just as Pauline had done. She thought it was cute to always have us in matching outfits. I resented this from the start and felt like I was her plaything. What was more worrying was that she dressed us as she herself dressed – like tarts. She wore skintight jeans and little tops with suggestive slogans on them, and she bought us tight trousers, little shorts and cropped tops. We looked older than we were and the clothes looked provocative. It was a completely different style from the conservative dresses we were made to wear at Pauline and Graham's.

In the years since leaving our birth home we had undergone different changes in appearance, from dressing like feral kids through two very distinct identities and, although at the time we accepted it, I can only imagine now that it would have had some sort of effect on Kirsten and me. We didn't know who we were or how we were supposed to act. Were we prim and proper Sunday School children, or precocious, pre-teen brats? Neither of us had been given the chance to develop our own tastes and identities because we were forced to take on those that were imposed on us.

The domestic set-up at Barbara's felt unstable. She didn't work so there was little routine. Paul lived elsewhere but spent a lot of time at the house and she was always overtly affectionate with him in front of us. He used to come round and watch horseracing on the television and, because Barbara did not drive, he would ferry her around everywhere.

It soon became apparent that David and Sharon did not have a great relationship with their mum. They often argued and would be out a lot of the time. I'm not sure what effect Kirsten and me arriving had on the family dynamic but we arrived with our own issues and challenges. We argued a lot and there always seemed to be tension in the air. Kirsten and I were left in the house with the adults and to remove ourselves from the inevitable atmosphere caused when there was an argument we used to play in the garden a lot, making mud pies.

The street was on a council estate and the next-door neighbours were not welcoming. They hated Barbara, would argue the whole time and, within a few months of moving in, Barbara had had a physical fight with one of them.

From that day on they had a vendetta against her and we were warned that we could not play in the street anymore in case we were attacked. Life at Barbara's soon became stressful, which is probably why she and Paul smoked the whole time. They even smoked while they were eating and didn't seem at all bothered that their habit could be affecting the range of health problems I had. My eczema and asthma were still bad and no one knew my full medical history because Terri had never taken me to a doctor. I had two inhalers for the asthma, a blue one and a brown one. Cold weather would trigger it and I'm sure the smoking didn't help. To this day, I still don't know if I ever had chicken pox as a child or whether I had any inoculations – there were no records. My breathing and skin complaints did not get properly checked out until I moved to Barbara's. I needed wet wraps for the eczema, which were full-length bandages dipped in a special solution. It was uncomfortable but did at least offer some relief from the continual itching, which was brought on by stress. I often scratched until my skin bled.

It soon became apparent that the woman who made the comical introductory DVD for us wasn't so nice as she and the social workers had made out. She had little patience with us and our behaviour. We could be challenging, there was no doubt about it – we had come from a very difficult background – but she couldn't sympathise. For example, I wet the bed frequently in those days and, whenever I did, I got scared and tried to hide it by turning the mattress over. Barbara could smell it so she told me off and smacked me. I wasn't even shocked – violence had been a regular fact of life, I thought it was what adults did to children.

Barbara's moods very quickly turned. Her face reddened, her voice rose and she would spit when she talked. She scared me. Often she didn't need to say anything, she delivered a withering look that made me feel like I was nothing. I couldn't understand why she wanted to adopt Kirsten or me – she didn't seem to like us very much. Barbara drank and she was unpredictable. She had the capacity to be nice but, even then, always there seemed to be a pay-off. She stroked my hair lovingly but then pulled it, jerking my head back. It was meant playfully, she would laugh while she was doing it, but to me it seemed spiteful. I never knew what she was thinking or what she was going to do next.

Barbara was preoccupied with her make-up and toiletries, and would often accuse me of stealing her shampoo – she had a thing about hair. She tied mine back very tightly and, when I went to school, she counted how many times the hairband had been tied to make sure it was secure. When I got home, she counted to make sure it had the same number of knots in it from the morning. I got headaches at school. Whenever she was angry, she constantly reminded me that she had done me a favour by taking me in.

The first Christmas we were with her I remember her putting empty bags in other bags and telling us they would have all been full of presents if we hadn't been so naughty. It was a strange way of teaching us a lesson. I woke on Christmas morning, excited by the bags, and tore through them while she watched. The more I opened, the more I started to resent her.

'That's what you get for being naughty,' she laughed. But then she pulled a gift from behind her and gave it to me.

'You don't think I'd give you nothing, do you?' she cooed, which made me feel bad for thinking she didn't get me anything. It was a form of psychological control.

Although Barbara was supposed to be our forever Mum, it was becoming increasingly plain that she was having trouble coping. As the months progressed, her relationship with her own children got worse and the rows and problems in the house became overwhelming. We all seemed to be arguing the whole time. Kirsten hated it and argued back. I don't recall lots of detail about the time; I was young and so much happened in the following years that many early memories are vague, but I have since seen documents from social workers that paint a detailed picture of the way the household fell apart and how Barbara was increasingly unable to cope. They describe 'testing misbehaviour, which included chewing furniture, and persistent, confrontational lying over comparatively trivial matters'. We were disturbed children and I'm not sure whether Barbara had been made fully aware of this; she was certainly not equipped to deal with it.

One report describes our first six months with Barbara. 'There were a number of problems with the girls' behaviour,' it states. 'Kirsten in particular frequently wet herself, sometimes by accident but also quite often deliberately. There were also acts of defiant disobedience and many examples of lying.' The report made it clear that Barbara felt I was the problem in the house. It goes on to give a description of what she told a psychologist she was seeing: 'She describes Lauren displaying persistent, negative behaviour and a refusal to accept discipline.' According to her, I was unable to concentrate; I was mean, destructive, disobedient, jealous, secretive, stubborn, moody and I hung around with troublemakers and stole things. I was eight years old at the time but I was no angel, and Kirsten and I needed specialist guidance to help us recover from the trauma of our early childhood.

The report detailed how, in 2000, the household disintegrated. Sharon moved out. First, Barbara blamed me, and then she blamed Kirsten. The arguments were becoming intolerable and no one seemed to be in control. Increasingly, social workers were becoming involved. Later I learned that Barbara and her children were called in for special counselling and that she had voiced concerns about going ahead with the adoption. The experts did not know the full extent of the problems she was experiencing with her own family at the time and had advised her that we were displaying normal boundary-testing behaviour. On two occasions, we were sent on temporary placements to other foster carers to give her respite.

Then, in June 2001, things came to a head. I've shut out much of what was happening in those months. At least with Terri and Shane I knew where I stood. If they were drunk, I would be hit and, if I was naughty, I would get a beating. But Barbara was erratic. Sometimes she would be normal, sometimes affectionate. Often she was overwhelmed. Paul didn't get involved. I think he was probably scared of her.

In the run-up to the event, things in the house had been getting worse and this made Kirsten and me increasingly anxious. We reacted by reverting to the testing behaviours the report highlighted. Barbara now found it impossible to control us. Kirsten was frequently wetting herself and, on occasion, soiled herself and smeared it all over the walls. She would also gnaw on the furniture. Both of us ripped wallpaper from the walls – we were acting like caged animals. Then, one day, Kirsten started rollerblading in the hallway. Barbara told her to stop. She refused and the argument became louder and more aggressive. Barbara then smacked Kirsten and, when she went up to her room, hysterical, David barged in and put a pillow over her face in anger.

Kirsten called social services and asked to be taken away. She fled, and they met her down the road. She was taken away and she never came back; she asked to go into care and live in a children's home rather than return to the house. In part, she blamed me for the problems that had been brewing for months.

The local authority also decided to take me away, but Barbara lodged a court action to formally adopt me. I didn't know any of this was going on in the background, all I knew was that I was stuck there, isolated and alone. I found out later when I saw my files. I had begun my childhood with parents and four siblings. Gradually, through the years, my family had all been whittled away until it was just me and a woman I was frightened of. At home, all the fight and defiance left me. I didn't argue, I was too scared. I did everything in my power to please Barbara, to try to be the good little girl she wanted. When I became compliant and withdrawn this pleased her.

At school it was a different matter. I had been a model pupil before Kirsten left. Teachers described me as popular, confident and pleasant. Almost overnight all that changed. Looking back on it as an adult, I realise that I was exhibiting the behaviours at school that I was forced to repress at home. I became argumentative and disruptive. Whenever I was thrown out of class, I would cry for ages out of frustration. I would get angry and confused; my moods swung wildly. In a court document relating to Barbara's attempt to adopt me, the headmistress described me as 'sullen, extremely moody and falling in and out of friendships on a daily basis'. I was spinning out of control but I didn't know who or what I was supposed to be.

Kirsten and I attended the same school and at first it was difficult because relations between us were strained. She was really angry with me. It was hard – I was so confused, she wouldn't speak to me. Outside of school I was left on my own with Barbara. I felt I had no one to turn to. In my early childhood, I had turned to my brothers for affection and, when we were split, it was my sister but after she left there was no one. I used to spend a lot of time alone in my room, hugging my duvet.

Gradually, however, Kirsten and I began to repair our relationship with the help of a support worker. Suzy was gorgeous, young and cool, and used to pick Kirsten and me up each week one day after school and take us out. She was assigned to help us maintain contact and work through our problems.

She would take us out places. We went swimming regularly and, through these visits, we learned to play together again. It was just my sister and me. We still had irregular contact with Terri and our brothers but these weekly outings were just for us. Suzy made sure they were as relaxed as possible.

While all this was going on, I was sent to stay with another couple, irregularly. It was usually once a week for a few hours. I was dropped off and picked up. For legal reasons I cannot go into detail, but I had known them for a while and they had looked after both Kirsten and me on many occasions. They were elderly and perfectly nice but, when Kirsten went and it was just me, things began to change.

They lived in a large house with a basement, which had been converted into the old man's workroom. He made wine there, tinkered with DIY, did some woodwork and generally pottered around. He spent a lot of time down there in the depths of the house and often Kirsten and I had helped him out.

A few weeks after she had gone, he called me down.

'I'm making jam,' he said. 'I could do with a hand.'

There was an old hob down there and I could smell sweet aromas drifting up, so I walked down the wooden staircase to join him. He sat me down next to him and put some empty jars in front of me and a saucepan of warm, stewed fruit.

'Fill those, please,' he said, passing me a spoon.

As I started scooping out the gloopy jam I felt his hand rest on my thigh. I was wearing a pair of the tight shorts Barbara liked me in and a T-shirt. As I felt his hand rise higher up my leg, I squirmed.

'All girls do it,' he said, 'there's no need to worry.'

He violated me and afterwards told me to be quiet about it because Barbara would never believe me if I told her, and she would be angry. That was the last thing I wanted. And although I knew what he was doing was not right, it was not the first time I had been abused. I believed it was what adult men did. When I got home I said nothing about it and so the abuse continued for several months. It always followed the same pattern: I was lured into the basement under a false pretext. After each time I became even more subdued and compliant.

But things were changing. Social services were aware of the chaos that had split up the fractured family I found myself in and were making concerted efforts to remove me from it. They had been speaking to my teachers and were closely observing the situation. Now they had come to the conclusion that the placement with Barbara was not going to work and would ultimately prove detrimental for me. I wish they had realised that before they sent Kirsten and me there in the first place. If only they had, then we might have been able to stay together.

At one stage I recall going to see a psychiatrist with Barbara. I didn't understand at the time and had been to see child psychologists and counsellors before so it wasn't a big deal. Many years later, I saw his report and it stated that I would never answer a question without looking at Barbara first for reassurance that I was giving the right answer. I was terrified that I would say something wrong.

The overriding memory I have of life with Barbara is that, although she fed and clothed me and was caring at first, she was unequipped to deal with me or Kirsten and the problems we had. When I think of Barbara I don't have good memories. I'm sure she thought what she was doing was right and I doubt she had any training to deal with emotionally disturbed kids so I can't blame her entirely. I'm sure social services thought they were doing a good job in finding us a home, but the placement leaves questions as to why Barbara was not assessed properly and how much information she was given about us.

In the end the council had to go to court to take me back into care. The system worked slowly. Eventually I was taken away: July 2002, just before my tenth birthday. But that didn't stop Barbara and she appealed against the decision. It took a High Court judge to ultimately dismiss her claim, and the case rumbled on for a long time after I left her. It was like a cloud hanging over my head and an added obstacle in the way of me finding a new forever family, although by that point I had started to realise that the word 'forever' did not necessarily mean forever.

Although I was vaguely aware all this was going on, I had no idea of the legalities. I wrote a letter to the judge saying I wanted to stay but the psychiatric evaluation concluded that I was being coerced. Barbara often reminded me how much she wanted me to be her daughter. She made a fuss of me sometimes and other times she got angry; she blamed me. I pretended I was sad because I didn't want to upset her but I was excited about going. It was the summer holidays and I knew I had time off school; I was like a prisoner coming to the end of a sentence.

When the technicalities had been dealt with and I was found another placement, I was given a week's notice. I wanted to be somewhere permanent, rather than having to be moved again. I'd had enough of being shuttled about, but I was told I was going to another temporary foster placement while the search continued for a parent.

When the time came to leave, Barbara wouldn't say good-bye. She didn't speak to me that day; she was too upset. Paul did; he wished me luck and I think he was sad to see me go. I gave him a hug. In the ensuing months, Barbara tried to keep in touch but in the end she was told to stop getting in contact as her attention was not helping me to move forward.

She would write me letters and sign them 'love Mum'. I'd called her 'Mum'. I called everyone I stayed with 'Mum' but I had no idea what the word meant.

Chapter six

THE KID WHO WAITED

A couple of months before I moved out of Barbara's house, one of the social workers I saw asked me to start compiling my life story. The idea was two-fold: social services would have a mini biography of me to show prospective adopters and I would also have the opportunity to reflect on my life and to come to terms with what had happened. Where do I start? I wondered. Shane's beatings? Terri's drink and drugs? Sexual abuse? Psychological cruelty? The loss of my brothers and sister? Inappropriate placements? I didn't get very far with it and the care system knew more about my life than I did anyway – I had blocked much of the difficult stuff out. In the end, the story was written for me and I later learned from my files that certain aspects were glossed over. I had reported the sexual abuse to counsellors I had been sent to and to social workers on different occasions but the allegations had never been taken seriously and were not included in the details about me that were sent to adoptive candidates.

After Barbara, I was sent to a lady called Karen in a nearby town. She was married to a man named John. She was supposed to be a specialist in difficult placements. It was well acknowledged that I needed dedicated care given my history, and Karen was deemed the best person available to provide it. And she probably would have been, if it wasn't for the fact that her marriage to John was on the rocks.

She was a decent person and the home she lived in was beautiful. It was in a cosy rural location and was warm, welcoming and picturesque. In the event, however, I didn't spend very long there. Instead, I ended up being bounced between two homes, staying most of the time with her husband in the house he moved into after their marriage broke down. As far as I know, social services knew none of this was going on. John was a very kind man and had the best intentions. He genuinely cared but he was completely unequipped to cope with a foster placement. He tried to look after me to the best of his ability in a difficult situation. There was no abuse and plenty of patience. His house wasn't ideal, it was small and it didn't have many toys or comforts in it, but I had been in far worse. He didn't prompt me to have showers and look after myself, which I needed at that age. I wasn't good at personal hygiene; I hadn't been taught. He didn't do things like check my hair for nits and, while I was with him, the scabies returned. He didn't know how to structure my time. He was a plumber and he took me out at night when he went on jobs. Sometimes it would be after 10pm. I loved it because he got me up and told me we were going out on missions. We would stop at Morrisons if it was open and get a chicken and mushroom pasty to eat on the way. It was fun but I should have been in bed, not sitting in a van.

Their marriage broke down a few weeks after I arrived but John had already got his own place by then so I assume their relationship had been troubled for a while. To their credit, if they did row, they kept it hidden from me.

Karen was a decent enough person but she was obviously going through some form of midlife crisis. A top-heavy woman, she wore clothes that clung to her and showed off her boobs.

The move to Karen's also meant a move to another school. By that stage in my life, I had already been to five different ones. I started one when I was still with Terri and Shane, I went to one when I was with Graham and Pauline, then another at Barbara's, during which time I had been sent on two respite placements. Throughout each of these I was required to attend a school for a few weeks near the places I was staying in order to maintain a level of attendance.

The school I started while I was at Karen's was the best I had been to. I began at the beginning of a term, which helped. It was always difficult trying to catch up when I was parachuted into a new school in the middle of a term. I had no problems making friends but it was hard to maintain friendships when I never knew how long I would be staying and, although academically I could read and write well, my maths was weak. But the staff at the new school had been made aware of my situation and they welcomed me and tried to make it as easy for me as possible. It was the only school where I made real friends. I always approached other kids and asked to play. I got on well with the teachers and the headmaster kept an eye out for me. On the first day, my form teacher assigned a friend to show me around. Her name was Charlie and we stayed friends after that. She was a lovely, feisty little thing with dimples and she was popular, so I made other friends through her.

My social circle grew when I was enrolled in a local social club for kids, and I used to love going there and hanging out with my friends. I had never had a social circle before. My brothers and sister had been the only other kids I played with regularly and we formed a protective pack when we were together. Unfortunately, however, being a child in care meant that there were some things that I had to be excluded from. I wasn't allowed to go on trips because I was classed as vulnerable and this caused problems one Sunday when the social club arranged a day out.

There was a bus booked to take the children to a local attraction and I desperately wanted to go. I asked Karen and she told me that I wasn't allowed to. I couldn't understand why and so I argued with her. She tried to explain and made the excuse that she couldn't afford the fee to save me from the reality that I was different from the other kids. I didn't believe her and, when the day came for the trip, I left home on my own and went to get on the bus myself. The club was in a hall a few minutes from Karen's house and, when I got there, the children were already lined up and filing onto the vehicle. I joined the queue.

As I went to climb up the stairs one of the organisers stopped me.

'Lauren, you're not allowed to go,' she said gently.

'It's OK, Karen will pay when she picks me up,' I lied.

But I was led off the bus while someone phoned Karen to come and pick me up. I started crying and, when she arrived, I threw a huge tantrum, screaming, thrashing about and refusing to go with her. One of the other organisers took pity on me.

'Let her go,' she said, 'I don't mind paying.'

Karen turned to her and within earshot of everybody else said, 'You don't understand. She can't go, she's a kid in care.'

Up until that moment, I hadn't told anyone at the club about my circumstances. I didn't make a habit of it. I wasn't ashamed; I just didn't want to be singled out. I wanted to be like all the other kids but, because of my circumstances, I needed permission from the council to go anywhere and, if I was going away or staying with another adult, they needed to be vetted. Mortified, I felt my cheeks redden. The bus stayed while Karen explained the situation to the organisers. I sat in the car, crying. Occasionally one of the adults in the confab would look over at me with pity. When Karen got in the car she apologised and tried to explain to me that it was for my own safety.

But I wasn't listening. I watched as the bus pulled away and saw my friends laughing and joking with each other. When we got home I told her that I didn't want to be with her anymore and ran into my room and hatched a plan. I was fed up and I wanted to run away from everything. It was December; cold and damp. I put on a couple of sweaters and the warmest trousers I could find and, when it grew dark, I crept downstairs, where I grabbed a packet of Jammie Dodgers from the cupboard and a torch. I got my coat, hat, gloves and scarf and sneaked out of the house.

I didn't know where I was going and wandered in the dark for about 15 minutes until I came to the park where I often played. There was a climbing frame in the middle of the play equipment, which had a covered shelter in the middle of it. I crawled inside and sat there, waiting to be found. The rain started after a while. It pattered gently off the wooden roof and dripped through the gaps. I pulled my hood up over my hat.

I was fully expecting someone to come and find me. I wanted Karen or John to rescue me and tell me everything would be OK. It got colder and darker. I was scared but determined not to give in. In my mind, it became a battle of wills.

At some point during the night, I curled up on the rubber safety surface of the park and fell asleep. No one found me; I assumed they were not even looking and that I hadn't been missed. I woke in the gloomy dawn light and decided to walk to the only place I felt wanted – the school. When I got there the doors were open and a couple of staff members were already there, preparing for the day. They found me a blanket and made me some food and a hot drink.

I didn't know it, but when Karen realised I had gone she had called the police and social services. There were police patrols searching for me and the police helicopter had been sent up to find me. John had been out all night, looking.

The teachers at the school were aware that I had gone missing and called the police, who came and got me and took me back to Karen. Though angry with me, she tried to be understanding; she told me it was unacceptable behaviour. It was the first time I had ever done anything like that and it caused a lot of worry. All my friends soon heard about it and many were quietly impressed that a 10-year-old could manage to evade a manhunt for a whole night by hiding under a climbing frame.

Then there was someone else who had been following the events closely, of whom I was unaware at that stage.

While I was getting on with life in limbo at Karen's, my details had been circulated among the adoptive community. At the time, there was a British fostering and adoption magazine called *Children Who Wait*. It was full of pictures and biographies of children who were looking for homes. My photo was printed in it with a description that read: 'After many sad disruptions and losses, Lauren is now ready to move to a forever family.' It said I liked Brownies, which I didn't, and mentioned that I had several siblings but that I was being placed on my own. 'Despite the disruptions she remains optimistic and cheerful,' it concluded.

Many miles away in Oxford a lady had seen the photo and brief details in the charity magazine and made enquiries about me. A single, professional, well-educated woman, she was totally different from any of the other people I had been placed with. She was well progressed along the adoption process. Unbeknown to me, already she had had several meetings with the social services department looking after me and had even been to Karen's house when I wasn't there. When I went missing she was called and informed and she waited, worried about my safety, until she heard that I had turned up, safe and sound. My disappearance and volatile behaviour did nothing to deter her. As she told me later, she believed I deserved the chance of a better life and she knew that, if she was going to take me on, it would not be an easy ride.

Her name was Elizabeth McDonnell. She decided she wanted to adopt a child because she had forgotten to have children herself. In her early fifties, she had never formed a permanent relationship. Her career had taken over and she was a bit of a workaholic. She worked at a very senior level in welfare policy with homelessness and the underlying cause. As part of her role, she had been involved in research into mental health, looking at why some people were more resilient than others and what could be done to help those who had bad starts in life. She became engrossed in the subject; she had done a lot of work around the effect on children in care and ways to improve their future prospects. She started to think about what she wanted to do for the rest of her career and decided to stop working and do voluntary and freelance work instead. Initially she considered fostering older teenage children, and when she was talking to someone about it they asked whether she had thought about fostering or adopting younger children. She assumed she wouldn't be eligible because of her age and the fact that she was on her own (she didn't realise that social services preferred to place older children with older single people). So she contacted a charity called Action for Children, which helped potential adoptive parents find children, and it went from there.

Through that organisation, she was vetted and counselled. She had been advised that it was better to go through a charity than a local authority and they did a thorough job. In January 2002, she started a formal legal process to become an adoptive parent. There were checks and visits, and training. She was formally approved in September of that year and started to look for a child. Later that autumn, she found me. By Christmas of that year, a few weeks after I ran away, she was told that the placement was likely to go ahead but the authorities decided not to tell me until after the festive season.

At the end of December, my case worker came to visit and explained that there was a woman who hoped to adopt me. She wanted to be my forever family and she lived in a city called Oxford. Then I was handed an album she had made for me. It was full of photos of herself, her family and her home; it also had photos of her dog. It was very well thought through, it was set out for me. 'This is me,' she wrote beside a photograph of herself. She looked kind and mumsy. I flicked through the pages. There was a photograph of a bedroom. 'This will be your room, but we can change the colour scheme if you want,' she wrote. The room had a sink in it, which I thought was amazing – I had never been given choices before.

'I like the look of her. I'd like to meet her,' I said.

I was keen – that had never happened before.

At each previous placement I had been passed around and had arrived with little choice. I wasn't given any opportunity to express myself, I never felt wanted. As soon as I saw the book, I felt Elizabeth would be different.

A contact was arranged and in January she came to visit me up at John's house. She drove for many hours in the snow and brought her dog with her – a tiny, yappy Terrier. She also had a cat. I loved animals and was thrilled at the prospect of going somewhere with pets. John had a massive Old English Sheepdog. By the time Elizabeth knocked on the door, I was really excited as I answered. I was smaller than she was expecting. She looked down at me and smiled. Her face was warm and friendly. She arrived early and had been waiting around the corner. I could tell she was nervous.

'Hello, Lauren,' she said.

The dog she was holding was squirming and managed to break free from her. It ran past me into the house where John's dog stood, startled. It barked and the Old English Sheepdog turned and ran out into the garden. We all laughed. John invited her in and we sat down among all the clutter of Christmas that hadn't been put away and chatted easily. She asked me about school and I told her about my friends and teachers, and my favourite subjects; she told me a bit about herself. Straight away, there was a connection. I had a good feeling about her.

Together with John, we went for lunch at the Toby Carvery. I had a long cowl-sleeved sweater on and the sleeves kept dropping in the gravy. We talked about our lives; she asked me about my brothers and sister and about my parents. With previous carers, it had been a subject that was usually avoided. I liked the fact that she acknowledged my past. After lunch we went for a walk in the snow.

It is safe to say that I loved the lady who became my mum from the first time I saw her. She had never fostered before, I was the first child she chose and she jumped in at the deep end. As we walked in the winter chill, I could tell she was hesitant about putting her arm around me. There were no hard and fast rules about boundaries and she was feeling her way. I went up and gave her a big hug; I thought she was lovely. I wanted to go home with her that day, I knew she was right – she didn't look like the sort of person who was going to hurt me. But the rules said we needed time to get to know each other and to make sure the placement was something we both wanted, and so, at the end of the day, she made the long journey back to Oxford.

But I had already made up my mind.

'Can I come with you?' I asked.

She shook her head kindly and assured me that we would see each other again very soon. I was sad when she went but, for the first time, I was filled with hope.

Chapter seven

MUM

Anyone can have a child but to be a mum takes thought, time and effort. And Elizabeth had worked hard to get to the stage where she was a potential mum. She had been approved by social services and, rather than passively pass through the system until all the boxes were ticked, she had been very proactive, making it clear what was expected of her and what support she expected.

She was the first person to raise my domestic circumstances with my case worker. She realised I wasn't living where I was supposed to be living: she had been told that I was living with Karen in Karen's house, yet when she visited I was with John. She was surprised but by then was starting to realise just how chaotic things had been for me and how chaotic the system for children in care was. That made her even more focused on adopting me. She found it odd that social services were not aware of my situation.

I've since learned that some people get involved in fostering and adoption for the wrong reasons. For some, who get an allowance if they look after a child, there is a financial incentive. Others want to concentrate on saving children to mask issues they themselves are working through. Elizabeth had thought an awful lot about what she was doing; she knew a lot about me by that point. She had met my schoolteachers and seen my bedroom at Karen's.

It wasn't long before we met again, and over the following weeks we had a lovely time getting to know each other. The second time I met her she drove up again and stayed at the nearby Holiday Inn for a couple of days. I stayed with her for the whole day until it was time to go back at night. She brought a huge art box and filled it with stuff she thought I might like to do. All I wanted was to play in the shower and run up and down the stairs, but she was fine with that. She couldn't get me to sit down and talk because I was so excited. I was dressed in a mish-mash of clothes and had children's shoes with heels. She was obviously still wary of my behaviour because I would go into the cafe on the ground floor to snatch sachets of sugar and at one point had disappeared for a while; she thought I'd run away.

We spent a lot of time in the hotel room. I wasn't fussed about going out so we stayed in, did some art and talked. Elizabeth wanted to know all about me, and I wanted to know about her. She asked what I liked, what I liked to play, what toys I liked. She never assumed anything. Whenever she spoke about the future she always said, 'If you did come and live with me'. But by then my mind was made up – I wanted to live with her.

During that time, one of our conversations turned to the subject of what I would call her. There was no pressure on me at all.

'If you do come and live with me, it doesn't matter what you call me,' she said. 'You can call me whatever you want.'

'I might as well call you Mum, because that's what you'll be,' I shrugged. It was so easy and, more importantly, it felt right. For the first time in my life, I felt I was conferring the title on someone who would actually take it seriously and who would work to earn it. From that moment on, Elizabeth McDonnell was my mum and I was her daughter.

The next step in our relationship was for me to visit her in what would be our home. Mum came and picked me up and drove me back to Oxford for a sleepover. Again, it was completely different from the previous placements; we were being encouraged to spend time together and to get to know each other. I was thrilled at the prospect of going to look around the house and town where I had already decided I was going to live. It was like going on holiday; I had never been so far south and I had never heard of Oxford.

When I got there it was amazing. Mum lived in a really nice part of Oxford and was surrounded by historic-looking buildings. I thought Oxford was a fantasyland with all the spires and picture-book buildings – there were even swans on the river. Her house in Oxford was a Victorian terrace. It was homely and to me it seemed huge, spread over four floors. I spent much of the time we had running up and down the stairs. It was cosy, especially on a cold winter's night. It felt very different to what I was used to and seemed very posh. Mum worked at the time – she was involved in voluntary work and she had a circle of well-to-do friends who all worked in charities, at the university and were people who commuted to London. They were well-educated professionals in decent jobs. The neighbours were teachers, lawyers and academics.

I hadn't been used to living with people who worked. It all felt solid and stable; it was also scary because I had never experienced anything like it before. I wondered if I would fit in. Before I met Elizabeth, part of me worried that I would just get bounced into another nightmare situation but, when I saw the environment she lived in and the life she lived, I realised this was not going to be the case. She seemed dependable.

During the period when we were getting to know each other, I had a planned contact visit with Terri. At that stage, I was only seeing her and my brothers three times a year. Mum never discouraged me from seeing her – quite the opposite. She thought it was important that, no matter what happened with the adoption, I should keep in contact with my birth family. The visit coincided with a day when Mum was with me so she came along to meet the rest of my family as my nan and granddad were scheduled to be there too. The meeting took place in a social services office. I took Terri a red rose. It was lovely to see Nan and Granddad but, as usual, Terri was hardly bothered.

'You alright then?' she asked dismissively. She hardly made eye contact.

There was no conversation. Several years later, Mum told me that, during the four contacts she attended between Terri and me, she hardly ever saw Terri speak to me, other than to make brief small talk. She would just ask if I was OK out of courtesy and that would be it.

Terri did do me one service after that meeting, however: she gave Mum her blessing. She liked her when they first met and told social services that she agreed with the proposed placement. It was the one good thing she did for me. The authorities also had a duty to ask Shane. I think he may have been in prison at the time because he wouldn't give an answer, so they overruled him and made the decision for him. In subsequent months when the adoption process was going through the courts, he kept missing court hearings because he was so unreliable. I assume he would have said no anyway as he always did.

Soon after that meeting with Terri I was told that everything had been approved and I was to start my new life with Mum in Oxford. I was overjoyed. For me it was a completely new start and filled with possibility.

The only aspect I was sad about was leaving the primary school I had started six months previously. I had settled in and made some good friends there. When I moved I was in Year Six and the move was going to happen in the middle of the term, halfway between Christmas and Easter. Mum came up to collect me on a Friday before the weekend of the move and had arranged a special surprise with the school.

She arrived early in the morning and took me in to school to say goodbye to all my friends. The head even said a few words during assembly and wished me good luck. Mum took a photo of me with my classmates before I left; she made a big deal of it. In all the other schools I had attended and left, I had never had a chance to say goodbye. I was there one day and somewhere else the next. By making a point of marking my leaving, Mum was making sure I felt valued. It was the hardest school to leave but also the best because I could see things would be different from then on.

I moved on 15 February 2003. When I left Karen's I had about half a dozen books and a couple of toys. It was the sum total of my life to that point. As a parting gift, Karen packed me off with 16 bin bags full of broken toys and clothes that weren't mine. It seemed a bizarre thing to do, and Mum later said she reckoned she took the opportunity to empty her loft and pretend that the rubbish she found in it was all mine. Although I was sorry to say goodbye to John, as he had been good to me, the excitement of starting a new life far outweighed any sadness.

On the journey south I was excited and didn't stop talking. We stopped on the way for lunch. Mum told me later that I looked like a ragged orphan – my clothes were filthy and I smelled. She didn't say anything at the time but she had to have the windows down. When we got home she suggested that it would be lovely to celebrate moving into my new home with a bubble bath. I wasn't too pleased because it wasn't something I was used to, but she persuaded me and, while I soaked in the water and washed, she got rid of most of the rubbish and dirty old clothes I had been sent with.

That weekend we had a moving-in party and Mum brought out a cake. She had placed a candle on top of it for everyone significant in my life. It was a lovely thing to do. Mum had gone to see a therapeutic worker who specialised in children and adoption, and she talked through how it might be for me when I first moved. That was when she was given the idea for the cake and candles – the thought behind it was to make sure I knew that the important people in my life would still be in my life and the door was not shut on them. As we lit each candle, we went through my birth family, former adoptive people, teachers and friends.

Meanwhile, I had a new family in Oxford. I had a new Granny and Granddad, two cousins, two uncles and an auntie. That first weekend we had a big family day at our house and afterwards we went to the nearby park. There was a lake inside the park, which had frozen over, and, while Mum was demonstrating how dangerous it was to walk on frozen ice, she fell through up to her knees. It was hilarious!

Mum had gone shopping before I arrived and filled my drawers with clothes. I had a hat and scarf, my own mirror and a mermaid soap dispenser.

The following weekend I was taken to Somerset to stay with Mum's brother, Uncle Michael, and his wife, Victoria. They lived on a farm and had horses. It was magical, but during the weekend Mum got a glimpse of the darker side of my behaviour. Up to that point I had generally been good, if not overly excitable, but there were still deep insecurities and unresolved issues in my mind that I didn't understand. I still had trouble accepting authority and was prone to mood swings.

On the Saturday morning, I was in the bedroom on the first floor of the farmhouse. Mum woke and came into my room to say good morning. There was a big, deep window set back in the thick stone wall and I was sitting on the window seat with the window open.

'I'm going to jump out,' I told her matter-of-factly and edged closer to the ledge.

I can only think I was looking for attention and, to her credit, Mum didn't entertain it.

'Oh well,' she shrugged. 'Breakfast is ready if you want it.' Then she walked out.

It was a random thing to say, and I think I was only doing it to try to work out how she would react. Despite my flashes of bad behaviour and the tantrums I sometimes threw, Mum was always patient and understanding.

My life in Oxford should have stayed perfect and for many months it was. After all, I was living in my ideal home with the mum I had always wanted. She was homely, loving and affectionate. There was more trust and security than I had ever experienced. At the weekends we did all sorts; our lives entwined. She expanded my horizons and took me to museums and to galleries. We were regulars at the Ashmolean Museum in Oxford and went to the museums in London; we spent hours in the Natural History Museum and I loved looking at the dinosaur bones; we went on long dog walks. I loved arcades and specifically dance machines. There was one near us and she used to take me on those and spend hours standing there, watching me.

I started a new school. Mum chose it even though it wasn't the nearest school to our house because it was smaller and was the feeder school into what she had been led to believe was one of the better secondary schools in the city. She was aware that given my background I would need stability and the secondary school she was hoping to send me to had a reputation for being a caring establishment. At primary school I flourished. I loved art, music and English; I was good at drawing and sketched a lot in my spare time. I learned keyboard. I made friends and Mum encouraged me to invite them round for tea and to play. When the time came to leave and start secondary school, she did everything in her power to persuade the local education authority to allow me to stay on another year. I was one of the youngest in my year group anyway and, up to that point, my schooling had been so disrupted she felt it would help me settle into my new life and give me stability. I completely agreed – I loved the school and felt safe there, I didn't feel ready to progress to secondary school. Unfortunately, however, the local education authority decided they knew better and told her that I would have to move up with the rest of Year Six, even though the head of the primary school supported her application.

The first summer I lived in Oxford we went to Devon and Cornwall on a traditional seaside holiday. We stayed with friends in Cornwall for the first week. They had a house overlooking the sea in a picturesque fishing village. During the second week we stayed in a caravan in Devon. I did things I had never done before such as swimming in the sea, body boarding and mackerel fishing; I got my hair braided, too. Away from everything I relaxed and the bond between us grew. For Mum it was a chance to see me have the kind of holiday she remembered enjoying as a child and a chance for her to show me off to friends. The official adoption hadn't gone through at that point as Barbara was still in the process of appealing against my removal so, even though I was living with Mum, she still had to seek permission to take me away. She was supposed to get permission every time we went away and, if she had any friends or family to stay at the house, she also needed to get permission for this.

Holidays became a big part of our life together and in the following years, as the troubles started, they became a way for us to reconnect. A year later, Mum took me abroad for the first time in my life. We went to stay at my uncle's house in the South of France. I was more excited about the prospect of flying in a plane than anything else and begged to sit by the window – a wish Mum was more than happy to grant. As the ground dropped away and the cars and houses got smaller and smaller until the plane punched through the fluffy white clouds and cruised off into the blue sky, I stared in wonderment.

I was filling up on the opportunities I had missed out on. It wasn't just foreign holidays, love and affection I had gone without for the first 10 years of my life, it was normality. In essence, I had missed out on being a child. Often I assumed it would all end and the dream would be over. Outwardly, I was confident and happy; inside I still had deep insecurities. I would wonder why Mum wanted me.

One day I asked her.

'Why did you choose me?'

Mum looked at me kindly.

'Because you looked like a lovely little girl who deserved a chance,' she said.

But I didn't believe I was lovely; at that time I didn't realise I had had a particularly difficult upbringing. I didn't reflect on things but somewhere inside there were unresolved issues caused by my turbulent early years.

I could be quite stand-offish, especially around adults I didn't know. I didn't want to make eye contact or talk, I wasn't trusting. I wasn't even trusting of Mum until I had tested her a few times to see how she would react to my moods and behaviour. I was more trusting of men than I was of women, which was strange when it was men who had let me down.

In theory, Mum should have known all about my background but, in reality, she only knew parts of my history. She was given a form before she chose me, which listed a whole range of issues a child in care might have faced, and was asked to rate them on how she felt she would cope. The issues were things like disabilities, mental health problems and physical neglect. The one thing she wouldn't know how to cope with, she said, was sexual abuse because she had no experience of it. They told her that it was not an issue with me. Even though I had reported it, all my life it had been brushed under the carpet; I was never believed.

Time passed. I started secondary school; we settled into a domestic routine. Still the legal adoption was dragging on and I became fixated on it: I wanted it to happen. I wanted to be free from my old life. It was around this time that I also started to ask to be called by a different name: I didn't like Lauren, I didn't like who she was or where she had come from. I'm not sure where the name Lara came from – I think I read a book with a character called Lara in it and decided that was what I wanted to be named. I asked Mum to call me Lara and whether it would be possible to change my name legally. She explained that if that was what I really wanted then, yes, she would call me Lara from then on but we should wait a while and see how I felt in a few years' time before permanently changing my name. If I really was sure that I wanted to formally become Lara in a year or so, then we could look into it.

The adoption process started to depress me. I worried that, until it was sanctioned by the courts, I wouldn't be staying. All the time I wasn't legally adopted I felt there was a chance I would be taken away again; I felt insecure. I was scared to get used to the stability until my place with Mum had been made official.

I moped around the house. It felt like the issue was hanging over my head. I became depressed and took to my bed but Mum came up with a plan to get me up again and back at school.

'So, are you well enough to go and get a puppy?' she asked.

I had been reading a book about puppies and was keen to have one of my own to look after. Mum knew there was nothing she could do about the court process but she could cheer me up with a distraction. I grinned at her.

'I've been doing some research and there is a breeder nearby,' she told me.

I got dressed and we drove to a nearby smallholding that unfortunately turned out to be not much better than a puppy farm. There were outhouses full of different breeds of dog. I didn't care, though – I wanted a dog like Mum's and immediately fell in love with one. A clumsy ball of fluff, he tripped over his bed and it flipped over on top of him. He wasn't the prettiest puppy I had ever seen but I didn't care: he had bags of character. He came home in my coat, with sawdust all over him. He had huge ears, which he eventually grew into, and we called him Snowy.

At home on the first day, he managed to climb into the chimney breast and came out black with soot. He was magical! Snowy slept in my room in a little puppy tent and he cheered me up enough for me to go back to school. At the end of the day Mum would come and pick me up with him in a bag. In a way, having Snowy proved to me that Mum was committed. I thought to myself that having a dog meant she couldn't get rid of me, even if the adoption didn't go ahead.

Thankfully, in March 2004, it finally happened. We were given notice that there would be a formal hearing in Birmingham and were invited to attend as a way of marking the day I officially became Mum's daughter. We made a whole day of it; we went up the night before and stayed in a hotel. Granny, Grandpa, Michael, Victoria and Mum's other brother

Gerry also came. There were two social workers and a lawyer in attendance too.

In the family court there was an official ceremony. Mum and I had bought outfits to wear – she helped me choose mine – and the judge announced that I was officially adopted. Then we all had our photo taken together and the judge let me wear his wig. I signed a certificate to say that I consented to be adopted. It was final, it was for real and, at that point, I dreamed the stability would last. The process had taken 13 months from the date I moved to Oxford. It went on and on. Throughout, Mum had been left largely on her own. I had shown testing behaviour at times and, while the support worker was always on the end of the phone, she was based in Birmingham. Once every six weeks a posse of people from social services descended on her to tick boxes and have review meetings. They would ask basic questions: Was I eating healthily? Was I in school? Mum told them about my behaviour and they agreed that I was testing her to see how she would react.

The first 18 months were not easy for her but they were what she had been expecting and we had lots of good times, getting to know each other. Neither of us knew what dark clouds were gathering on the horizon.

Chapter eight

SCHOOL'S OUT

On the surface everything looked normal. At home I had structure and routine: I came in from school and did any homework that needed to be done before the television went on. Mum and I had supper together; sometimes I would help her cook. I then had a bath and went to bed – it was all very normal. Perhaps that's why things started to go wrong. I didn't know what normal was. It was unfamiliar and alien. I loved Mum and respected her but I found being told what to do difficult. She liked to sit at the table and eat and talk without having the telly on in the background; I didn't. She also encouraged me to change my clothes every day, which I didn't like doing. She would leave clean clothes out for me and sometimes I would put them on over my dirty ones from the day before. At other times, I would try to get into bed with my day clothes on. Mum was very laid-back in most respects but it was things like cleaning, hygiene and wearing clean underwear that she was fastidious about. With me she needed to have different boundaries because of where I had come from. I had never been shown how to keep myself clean and presentable so she had to take extra care in making sure I bathed regularly, cleaned my teeth and brushed my hair, especially as I was going through puberty when those things are so important. I thought she was nagging but she was just doing what a mother should; her priority was getting my self-confidence up.

After the legal adoption, I was permitted to have friends over for sleepovers without them needing to be vetted and Mum allowed me to play out so long as I was home by 7.30pm. Even though her boundaries were perfectly reasonable, I always tried to push them.

I would start arguments over the slightest thing and blow them up to ridiculous proportions. At other times I would be rash and dangerous. I would try to hurt her with words. Once, just before I started secondary school, I told her that she was the worst mother in the world and that I just wanted to go back and live with Terri. She wasn't, and I didn't, but I craved a reaction from her. Another time we were driving along one of the main carriageways in Oxford and I opened the car door and threatened to jump out onto the concrete. Mum quite rightly flipped and told me how unacceptable and dangerous such behaviour was.

I always knew when I had upset her, though and knowing this upset me. I was confused by the way I acted. After one argument Mum had to go out so we got in the car and drove off together in silence. There was an awkward atmosphere in the car. She pulled up at the local store and got out to buy some dog food. She left me in the passenger seat and, while she was gone, I noticed a pack of Post-it notes and a pen in the glove compartment. I felt so guilty about causing the row that I scribbled the word 'sorry' on as many notes as I could and stuck them all over the inside of the windscreen and the side windows. I knew I was in the wrong, but I didn't want to verbalise it – it seemed easier to write my apology down. She hugged me when she saw what I had done; she was always ready to forgive.

Around the time I was 12 years old I went through a phase of ripping up photos – I did it to try to get a reaction. There would be an argument and I'd disappear to my room, where I'd pull out photographs of Terri and of my brothers and sister and start tearing them apart, before throwing them in the bin. I did it because I wanted a reaction from Mum, but, in reality, it upset me more than her. When I had calmed down or locked myself in my room in a sulk, Mum would quietly pick up all the pieces and carefully store them for me – she always believed that I should keep mementos of my past because one day I might want them. She continued to encourage me to see my birth family, even though often I didn't want to do so. After the adoption there was talk of me having six contacts with Terri a year but that would have been impractical and it remained three times a year: one at every school holiday.

'It is really important,' she would explain. 'Your relation-ships with your brothers and sister are for life.'

The destruction of property became a pattern whenever I felt frustrated. If we had an argument and I was upset or cross, I would do things that upset me but that I also thought would upset someone else, such as throw my laptop. Mum tried her best to stop me from doing it.

Within a few months of moving I had started secondary school and in the first year everything went reasonably well. It was a comprehensive in Oxford, which Mum chose because she had heard good reports about it. Before the first day of term, I went for an induction with other children from my class in primary school. We got to try sample lessons and meet the teachers and the other children. It was daunting. The school seemed huge but, having moved around so often, I was confident that I could cope with the change. And I was thankful that, for the first time in my school life, I would not be the only new face in the classroom. I started with a whole new year group; I was more worried about the older kids because I had goofy teeth and I feared being bullied.

Although I tried hard to begin with, after a year I started to struggle. It's a difficult time for any kid. I was going through puberty and was struggling with moods. With the benefit of hindsight I know there were many unresolved issues from my past coming back to haunt me. I developed an attitude problem; my moods changed in the blink of an eye. One minute everything was fine, the next, for reasons I didn't know or understand, I would get angry or very down. It didn't help that I was an early developer and hormones were amplifying my confusion. Though emotionally naïve, I was growing into a woman.

Puberty presented me with problems I felt unequipped to cope with. I don't remember anyone ever giving me the talk about the birds and the bees; I didn't know how relationships worked. Mum tried to talk to me but it's not easy for someone who has never had a child to communicate such personal stuff to someone who has come from an abusive background. When she started to broach the subject I cut her off quickly.

I started my periods before I moved in with Mum, but they stopped for a while and started again soon after I moved in with her. I freaked out when it happened. I thought I was dying. No one had ever discussed the subject with me and Mum assumed that I had already been told but I didn't know what was happening to me. I didn't know about growing up; I was frightened.

Mum assured me that what was happening to me was normal. But she hadn't expected it yet – after all, I was only 10. Once we got over that, I felt I was a grown-up and I had to act like one. It's a big benchmark in a young girl's life.

I started secondary school when I was 11. In the first year, Year Seven, I tried hard but by Year Eight I was starting to have problems. Academically, I was trying hard. I was good at English and my favourite lesson was design and technology. I liked using the tools, especially hammers, because they gave me the chance to vent some of the anger I often felt bubbling up inside me. However, I struggled with maths and was embarrassed by my lack of numerical skills. In every maths class the teacher always seemed to pick me out to answer questions, which made me defensive.

My attitude started to change. I had a volatile temperament – I felt like I was bullied by the teachers and then some of the older pupils began to pick on me as well. They would make cutting comments about my teeth. Then they found out where I came from, and they started picking on me because of that. I began to fight back and I started to dread going into school – I hated it.

No one seemed to be there to listen to me or to ask why my behaviour was on such a steep, downward descent. In primary school I had always been given a lot of support, especially as I was inevitably the new kid in class, but in secondary school it was sink or swim. It didn't matter what your issues were, you were expected to do everything on your own and I had trouble coping. There were a lot of expectations and I couldn't handle them. Over the years I had become so used to disruption that finding myself in a normal situation with a bunch of kids who were all in the same boat threw me: I felt uncomfortable being comfortable. The same thing was happening at home – I had spent so many years in flux, expecting things to change, that I found stability hard to deal with. All the time I would test to see what Mum's breaking point was; I wanted the adrenaline rush of an argument.

One of the people I turned to for support was my best friend, Jennifer. She came up with me from primary school and was in the same form as me; she lived with her mum. Jennifer was a strange girl: from a young age she was always very promiscuous. She knew all about boys and she was very well developed; she looked a lot older than she was, she had olive skin and big boobs but was slim. Jennifer would talk to older guys and, even at 12 years old, she would flirt with them.

I looked at her and I saw a grown-up. She spoke like an adult and I thought she was so cool. She had lots of boyfriends; she was always talking about them and would encourage me to go and meet them with her. I found it all really exciting.

Jennifer would get served in pubs and she could get into nightclubs from her early teens. She was almost left to her own devices by her family. Although she was never aggressive, I always got the impression her mum was scared of her. She didn't want to upset her, so she let her do as she pleased and she was intimidated by her. Jennifer was never grumpy; she was always smiling.

I met her on my first day at primary school. Jennifer was the first person to come up to me and say hello. She looked so out of place, like an adult wearing a primary school uniform. She looked years older than the other kids and, as the years progressed and we started secondary school together, she began to open avenues to me that excited me. She showed me another world. We were at an age when all the girls were beginning to show an interest in boys but, with Jennifer, it wasn't boys, it was men. She would describe a boyfriend she was seeing and throw into the conversation that he had a beard.

Jennifer had a camera phone, which I thought was cool. In Year Six when we were both still at primary school, she had shown me a picture of a man on it. She was with him in the photo and they had their arms around each other. She told me his name was Jay, that he was her boyfriend, he lived in London and he was a radio DJ. I had no reason to disbelieve her – Jennifer didn't tend to do a lot of lying. The following year, when we were in secondary school, she invited me to go on the train with her to London to meet Jay, which I did.

He must have been in his late twenties; she was 11. It didn't shock me at the time. I don't know why but there wasn't a lot that shocked me, given what I had witnessed and experienced in my early life. At that point, I was still naïve about men: I had never had a boyfriend. When I was seven, I had a friend called Steven and we would hold hands in the playground but I never got involved with boys until I started hanging around with Jennifer. It was then that I started to think that I wanted to try new things and see new people.

Jennifer had a motto at secondary school. 'You're only young once,' she would say before going off to meet a man. It was a strange thing for a 12-year-old to say. She would boast about being sexually active. The thought of having sex terrified me; I couldn't understand why anyone would want to do so willingly because in my experience it only caused physical and psychological pain but Jennifer seemed to revel in the fact she was leading an exotic, exciting and dangerous life.

Time moved forward and we both passed another birthday. At 13 I went for a sleepover at her house and another of her boyfriends was there. He stayed the night with her. He had driven to see her, so he was obviously over 17 because he had a driving licence. She never mentioned ages but he looked to be in his twenties. We went to her room to watch a DVD together and at one stage in the night her mum came in with a tray of sandwiches for us all. Jennifer and her boyfriend sat on the bed, snogging, and I sat on a blow-up mattress on the floor doing my best to ignore them. I fell asleep but woke in the middle of the night. I could hear them having sex. Half-asleep, I remember feeling uneasy about it and wondering if I was dreaming. The next morning, when I was fully awake, I realised what they'd done with me in the room and I was appalled. I shouted at Jennifer but I didn't really understand what was going on, and I was more annoyed at being woken up. She laughed and didn't mention it again.

I knew what she was doing was wrong; I knew the age gaps were inappropriate – I thought it was disgusting. Whenever she'd introduce me to one of her boyfriends I told them she was underage. It never put them off and although I used to get cross about it, Jennifer thought it was funny.

As we grew older, she would dress increasingly provocatively. Her belly was always showing and she wore tight clothes that showed off too much flesh. She wore make-up and clothes more fitting for someone in their twenties, but she had a child's face.

She always tried to encourage me to meet boys with her and I really didn't want to at that age. I knew nothing about sex apart from what had happened in the past; I always tried to avoid the thought or talk of it.

Despite Jennifer's grown-up façade, underneath it all she was still a child and often acted like one. We used to walk around the playground together singing and pretending we were going to go on the *X Factor*. Jennifer got bullied, too, and I started to defend her because I didn't like seeing people picked on – it reminded me of the way Shane had treated Terri, my brothers and sister and me. We made a good team.

Jennifer would often take herself up to London on her own to meet one of the men she was seeing, and on occasion I went with her. I never told Mum what I was doing and it was exciting. She had a circle of friends much older than school age and she introduced me to the other side of Oxford, where the tour buses didn't stop. These were the council estates and rundown areas away from the dreaming spires. It was the underbelly of the city, filled with drug dens and dealers, runaway kids and troublemakers. I wasn't scared of these rough areas: I had grown up in places similar to them, they felt familiar.

In December 2005 Mum's father, my adoptive grandfather, was becomingly increasingly ill. He had fought a valiant battle against cancer and Mum was spending more and more time with him as he neared the end of his life. It was a very sad time for her. A few days before Christmas she received a call from her mother, who said he was dying. Mum drove to Lincoln to be with him and my granny in his final hours. It meant leaving me alone and so she arranged for me to go and stay at Jennifer's for a few nights. She had no idea how unreliable Jennifer's mum was and assumed she had made the right decision, given the short notice and the difficult time she was facing. She dropped me off and arranged to keep in regular contact. Thirteen years old and impressionable, I went off happily to stay with my friend. Jennifer always wanted to do grown-up things, which I thought was cool and, when she said she wanted to go and meet her boyfriend at his home that night, at first I was reluctant but then curiosity got the better of me and I agreed.

Her boyfriend was called Abassi. He told her he was a student. She had met him one day while she was walking around the town. He had approached her and started talking to her. She got a lot of attention from men when she was out – they always seemed to be the same kind of men, usually black or Asian and often seedy-looking. Abassi lived in a place called Wood Farm. It was a shabby council estate, built in the 1950s and 60s to house workers at the car plant in nearby Cowley. As we walked there, she said we were going to watch a DVD and mentioned that Abassi's brother, Michael, might be dropping in later. I sighed. She had introduced us in the past and she was intent on trying to fix me up with him; she wanted me to lose my virginity to him. I wasn't sure how old he was but he looked about 40. The idea repulsed me.

'No way,' I said.

'I don't know why you are so against it,' she pressed. 'He's OK and it will be fun.'

'I'll go with you but I'm not getting involved in any of that,' I sighed.

Jennifer had covered herself in make-up; she wore heavy mascara and lipstick. Despite the cold, she chose to wear a skimpy top and short skirt. She was excited about getting out of the house and had left without explaining to her mum where she was going and when she would be back. It was obvious what she was looking forward to.

I assumed we were only going for a few hours and usually, when I went out, I called Mum to let her know where I was going. That evening I had enough sense not to call her because I knew where she was and I didn't want her to worry: already she had enough to contend with.

When we got to the flat, Abassi opened the door. He looked Jennifer up and down hungrily. He gave me the creeps, but I thought he was harmless. I couldn't understand why Jennifer was so into him, though. When he stood aside to let us in, he patted her bum suggestively. We sat around chatting. There was only one room with a bed in it, a TV and a DVD player. Jennifer and Abassi sat on the bed. His hands were all over her and they started kissing. I watched the telly. After a while, his brother came in. Michael was a big, muscular man, much older than his brother. He sat next to me and touched my leg. I moved away and he laughed. He tried to smooth talk me: he told me how pretty I was and that he fancied me. Although I didn't think I was in any danger, I didn't feel comfortable and so I told him I wasn't interested. Jennifer wasn't bothered – she had got under the covers with Abassi. I told her I wanted to go.

'Don't worry,' she said. 'We'll just stay for a bit.'

Eventually, Michael got the message and left, leaving me on my own on the floor watching TV while Jennifer and Abassi were in the bed. I was worried about her, whether they were using protection and whether she would get pregnant. I didn't think about my own safety; I knew where I was and where to go if I needed to get out. I always thought about where the door was in any situation – I'd learned to always be aware of the exit from the days when I would have to flee from Shane and his violent onslaughts.

I still thought we were going back to Jennifer's, but as the time went on I realised she had no intention of going home. I worried that I would get in trouble if Mum found out. Hungry and tired, eventually I felt myself dozing off. When I woke up it was Christmas Eve. Jennifer and Abassi were asleep in the bed and I made enough noise to rouse them. When she surfaced from the covers, I told her we should be going and that we would be in trouble. Abassi didn't seem at all bothered. Looking back now, it seems staggering to me that a man could happily spend the night with two children, have sex with one of them and just act like it was the most natural thing in the world. I don't doubt for one moment that he knew Jennifer was underage – I had already told him but it didn't seem to matter.

Jennifer could tell I was unhappy and so she collected her stuff and said goodbye. As we walked out, she told me to relax. Annoyed with her for making me stay out, I told her that I was going to find a phone to call my mum and stormed off.

The only place I could find that was open so early was a launderette. I dialled Mum's mobile.

'Where are you?' she asked urgently. 'Where have you been?'

'I've been at Jennifer's,' I lied.

'No, you haven't,' she said. 'I called her mum and she said she hasn't seen either of you and doesn't know where you are.'

I tried to change the subject.

'How's Granddad?' I asked.

'He died last night,' she said, her voice cracking.

My heart sank in my chest. How selfish had I been? While Mum had been watching her father die, I had been a runaway. I felt awful.

'Where are you?' she repeated.

I told her where I was and asked her to come and pick me up. When she arrived, she sighed when she saw what I was wearing. Like Jennifer, I had tried to dress like an adult. I still had last night's make-up on and I looked bedraggled. Mum asked what had happened and I told her I had been to a party and there were lots of people there. She didn't believe me, but I persisted with the lies and apologised for staying out all night.

Despite losing my grandfather, we still managed to have a lovely Christmas Day and we concentrated on supporting Granny. Mum must have been hurting so much inside but she made sure Christmas was still magical.

In the months that followed I started to become increasingly badly behaved. I don't know why. Hormones? Unresolved issues? Probably a bit of both. I became defiant, I started smoking; I didn't want to be in school and I was aggressive while there. I got into fights, and started staying out more; I was a brat. I was being naughty and pushing the boundaries to see how far I could stretch them. I ran away regularly, sometimes on my own and sometimes with Jennifer. We were not running away from anything, we loved home and we loved our families. We weren't doing drugs or drinking but it was exciting to stay out.

I would climb out the window and go off to meet my mates. Mum would call the police and report me missing. She told me off when I got back. It happened once or twice a week; it was fun – I would walk the streets and be a yob. Mum locked the windows but I chiselled the locks. Sometimes when she was asleep she hid the keys under her pillow, but I waited until she drifted off and sneaked in to try to get them. She would wake up and catch me with my hand under her pillow. I just giggled and ran off but would try again later. It was a game – I liked to wind her up. I never went out to cause trouble, or to hurt or fight or steal; I just wanted to go out at night and walk around like a grown-up. There was nothing sinister in it; I would stay out for an hour and come back because I got bored. The problem then was getting back in because I had climbed out a window that was higher up, so I had to wake Mum up.

I remember feeling guilty; I wasn't misbehaving to be nasty. By now I had a phone of my own and so I called Mum and annoyed her when I was out. She would ask if I was coming home and I would say, 'No, I am having fun.' Then she would ask if I had eaten. When I told her no, she would try to entice me back. 'I'll cook you something,' she offered. She was desperate to get me home and safe, but I thought she was being a nag.

I also started to dress in clothes that were much too old for me. Just like Jennifer, I began to get approached. Men would come up to me in the street when I was with Mum and try to chat to me. I was friendly in return. Mum chased them off and told them how young I was.

Sometimes it felt like I was two different people: one moment I could be loving and obedient and good, then I could spin off the rails, run away and become aggressive. I liked grime and R&B but I also had a crush on Bradley from S Club 7 – I had posters of him on my wall. I loved the children's TV programme *Art Attack* and I would sit in my room and make up a whole game around it, where I was the presenter. Other days I disappeared to Wood Green and would hang out with Jennifer and older men. I didn't know who I was supposed to be: there was a battle going on inside me between the good, innocent girl who wanted love and stability, and the bad, aggressive girl who craved danger and instability.

And the bad half was winning.

I was rapidly losing interest in school. Although I tried to be a good pupil and I enjoyed certain lessons such as art and English and I did want to learn, increasingly I was finding it difficult to obey the teachers. I had no respect for authority and would not follow rules – I answered back, I swore, I talked in class, I was argumentative and I disrupted lessons. I got my first detention for talking in class and, although I didn't get many more, the ones I did get were for talking or being rude.

Although I was starting to build a normal life with Mum, there was a part of me that was not satisfied and wanted to disrupt that normality. Understandably, I had issues but there seemed to be little acknowledgement of this in school – I felt that I was left to get worse, unchecked. There was no help offered. As far as I could tell, I was written off as a naughty child.

Towards the end of my first year in secondary school, I had my first fist fight. It marked a turning point in my school career. With hindsight, it was the beginning of the end. I was still being bullied at the time because of my teeth and I was always defensive. It was a hot day and I was in the playground, chatting to a few of my friends. Two Asian girls walked past and as they did they started picking on me in front of the other children.

I could feel the anger rising inside me like a red tide. Furious, I ran after them. I didn't think, I reacted; it was subconscious. When I caught up with them I lashed out with my fists. It was pure primal rage as I continued striking out at them. A crowd gathered round and began chanting, 'Fight! Fight!' This spurred me on. I'm not sure if they hit me back. If they did, I didn't feel anything. It felt like a release and I'm ashamed to admit that I enjoyed the feeling of empowerment I got. I was in such a frenzy that I don't even know how it ended. It lasted all of five minutes and in the end they fled, I think. But I wanted to carry on. I shouted abuse after them and some of the older boys had to restrain me until I calmed down.

A day later I was called in to the head teacher's office. I was expecting a reprimand. Fighting wasn't tolerated at school but I thought, whatever the punishment, it would be worth it because I had stuck up for myself and given the bullies a message.

What the head told me shocked me.

'We are investigating a racist incident,' he said. 'It's a serious matter, Lauren.'

Both the girls were Muslim and were wearing headscarves. During the brawl, their scarves had fallen off. They had accused me of pulling them off on purpose. I was horrified – I would never do such a thing and I was in no way racist. In fact, I never saw race or religion in anyone; I took each person I met on their merits, regardless of who or what they were. Tolerance was a deep-seated belief of mine. Shane and Terri were both racists – they were always ranting about blacks and Asians, even though we grew up in a multicultural area. They hated anyone who was different and I didn't want to be like them. And Mum was the most tolerant and accepting person I knew. Our household was completely open-minded.

Although I pleaded my innocence, I was suspended for a week while the school made further enquiries. I was upset by the whole episode; not because of the fight or the suspension but because there was a suggestion I had fought with the girls because they were Asian. Eventually, the school decided the motivation was not racist but I was warned to control my temper.

But I found it hard to keep a check on my emotions: everything made me angry, I could switch from laughter to rage in the blink of an eye. If I didn't get my own way or if I saw something I didn't agree with, I flew off the handle. Looking back, it is now obvious that the violence I had witnessed in my early years was having an impact on me and influencing my behaviour. I knew that I would get some sort of reaction by being violent, just as Shane did when he behaved in the same way. He got a reaction from us – fear – and this in turn gave him power.

That fight was to change my circumstances at school. Afterwards the bullies left me alone and I earned a grudging respect from them. The other kids began to look up to me and I started to become someone the other pupils went to for help if they were being bullied. I didn't want anyone to be scared of me, instead I saw myself as a protector and as someone people could depend on, so I fought people's battles for them and stuck up for those who couldn't stick up for themselves. A loyal friend, I always jumped in to help people I knew but this attitude simply marked me out as being even more of a troublemaker. Mum started to become aware of my problems at the end of Year Eight when she got calls from the teachers. She would question me about them and try to find out what was causing this change in behaviour and attitude but I refused to talk and would blame the school and the teachers.

Around this time I began skiving school. I started by skipping individual lessons and progressed to truanting for entire days; I didn't care about the consequences. Mum tried to entice me back to school with a series of rewards.

'If you manage a full week, I'll take you to the cinema,' she tried.

But it made no difference to me. I lost interest – I didn't believe the school had anything to offer me and they, in turn, didn't seem at all bothered about keeping me there. In reality, they didn't know what to do with me. I started being temporarily excluded in December 2004, which I thought was great – I didn't want to be there so they were reinforcing my behaviour by telling me to stay away. In the end, I attended a special behavioural unit, which was run by a lovely teacher called Mr Harris, one of the only ones who made an effort to understand me. He was old, approaching retirement, while most of the other teachers were brash and young, but he had time to spend with the troubled children in his care. He was the only one who showed an interest and understanding that I had been adopted and hadn't been in Oxford for long.

In the unit, we had our own room. I was in there with a bunch of people who were worse behaved than me, around six of us. Classes were for two-and-a-half hours a day, but, by the time Mum came to pick me up at 12.30, I was usually gone. I didn't worry about getting chucked out of school, I wasn't scared of anything. I never had an eye on the future: I had no plans, no aspirations, no interest in anything.

When I bunked off I hung out in the park with a group of other kids who always seemed to be there, smoking, swearing and messing around. Some were from my school, others from the various schools in the town and many of them didn't go to school at all. I was one of the youngest. They ranged in age from around 11 to late teens; I thought they were cool. None of them seemed to be bothered about being seen. My days were spent hanging around with the crowd and reluctantly going to lessons.

The event that ended my school career happened in the spring of the second year. I was in class and I was being disobedient. The class was being taken by a female teacher who eventually tired of my interruptions and told me to leave the room. I refused because it was my favourite lesson, design and technology. We had a standoff during which she became increasingly agitated and I grew more and more abusive and aggressive. Following this, she tried to physically remove me from the lesson and grabbed hold of my arm. She had long, false nails, which dug into my arm. I squirmed and told her to let go, but she tightened her grip and tried to drag me to the door. As I pushed her away, her nails dug deeper into my skin.

The red mist descended. No matter how much I tried, I couldn't free myself from her grasp. I lashed out at her. She let go of me and I stormed out.

Immediately I knew that I had gone too far. The school said they had no option but to exclude me while they tried to find other alternatives. I was never formally kicked out because, if they had done so, they would have had to come up with an alternative plan. Instead, I was left in limbo.

I felt strangely satisfied when I was removed. The whole episode reinforced a deeply held belief that things would always go wrong for me. I believed it was inevitable – there was always a part of me waiting for the drama and the instability. I didn't realise I was causing things to go wrong; I believed they happened to me, not because of me.

At school I never felt like I belonged. I felt different from the other children. Perhaps it was because I was adopted? I kept quiet about my past – I didn't want my peers to know that my birth parents were crazy. They all seemed to have normal parents and normal homes. Mine were not. Although

I now had a lovely mum, there was always a shadow in my past, and I was embarrassed by it.

I never told anyone about the sexual abuse because I had never been believed.

Chapter nine

OUT OF CONTROL

I was open to trying anything. I had no sense of proportion and no self-preservation mechanism so I never did anything in moderation. A prime example was the first time I got drunk.

I was around 13 and I was with a friend, Jo. She had to look after her 10-year-old sister for the afternoon and they came round to my house. Mum was out preparing for a party we were having – I think the occasion was her birthday. Because of this, there were lots of bottles of wine in the house.

'Let's have one?' I suggested to Jo.

She refused but I went ahead anyway. I had never stolen from Mum or drunk before, so she assumed there was no reason to lock the alcohol away.

I glugged from the bottle just as I remembered Terri doing. After I finished one, I started another. The effects hit me quickly; I became increasingly excitable. Somewhere during the third bottle I lost all concept of reality and can't remember anything. I only have details from what I have since been told. At some point I ran out of the house into the street.

I was staggering around in the middle of the road, manically shouting. I threw the bottle I was holding and it smashed onto the pavement; I fell down next to it and started drinking what was left from the broken glass. I ran up to strangers and grabbed them.

At some point Mum came home to find me wandering in the middle of the road. It was daylight, thankfully, and the drivers of the cars on the busy road could see me and were swerving around me. There was blood on my face from a cut. Mum tried to get me but I turned wild, lashed out and screamed at her before running off through the traffic. She called the police because I was unapproachable. Within minutes a squad car arrived, with its blue lights flashing, and the officers managed to grapple me into the back and belt me in. I was thrashing around and mumbling incoherently. They took me to the station with Mum following and could only think to lock me in a cell to dry out. As the door clanged shut, I screamed and shouted and ran at it repeatedly; each impact jarred my body. I fell and slammed my head on the floor but felt nothing.

After a few hours, they let me out. I was still aggressive and rambling but they sent me home, brusquely helping me out the door into Mum's car. When we got to the house, Mum tried to calm me down. Our neighbour, Jean, heard the commotion and came over to try to help. A good friend to Mum and a support throughout everything that happened during the subsequent years, she had a partner who didn't live with her and also had two girls. She was a nurse and cared about other people. Jean would hear our arguments and come in to try to help. Over the years there were times when she came round and literally had to sit on me to restrain me. Eventually she and Mum persuaded me to lie on the sofa, but, as I calmed down and faded into unconsciousness, I started to convulse and fit. Again, the emergency services were called and I was taken to the hospital, where I was scanned. It was discovered that I had sustained a broken hip and concussion. I was kept in for several days. That was my introduction to alcohol and I didn't touch a drop for many months after that.

Around the same time I had started to attract a lot of attention from men, especially older men. Even with make-up on, I looked my age, though. I don't know what vibes I gave off and it was nothing consciously but a certain type of man seemed to gravitate towards me. I was smiley and friendly and I think that was perhaps construed as being flirty. Easily approachable, I talked to anyone.

Being with Mum didn't put them off. Once we went to B&Q and I wandered off while Mum was looking at something. After a few minutes, she came to find me and discovered me in another aisle, talking to one of the employees. He was an old man, probably in his fifties, and he was trying to swap numbers with me. Mum was furious.

'Do you realise how old she is?' she called out.

Despite Mum's best efforts, my clothing style had started to change. Automatically, like most young teenagers, I thought that whatever she chose for me was old-fashioned and instead I looked for clothes that I thought Jennifer might like. I had a tendency to buy things that were too tight and too short, possibly a hangover from the way I was dressed by Barbara. When I was with Mum I wore normal things such as T-shirts, jeans and trousers, but, when I was with friends, I started wearing short skirts and skimpy tops. I also wore a lot of make-up. I thought I was grown up, but I was emotionally immature: I was a woman-child.

Mum struggled to hold on to my childhood. After all, I had barely had one and missed out on so much and yet, at 13 and going on 14, I was trying everything I could think of to grow up and be an adult. Throughout my life, adults had chipped away at my innocence. Lumps of it had fallen away, thanks to neglect and abuse. Mum tried so hard to keep what was left intact but, in the summer of 2005, another chunk of it was ripped away.

I was out with Jennifer. I'd had an argument at home – Mum had friends round and I was misbehaving. One of them told me off for doing something. As a result I flew into a rage and stormed out. I met up with Jennifer and we wandered into town. She had been seeing a man and she wanted to go and find him. Her relationships were not forged in the normal way; she was picked up by men who hung around in dodgy parts of town. There was no romance and courtship – they'd ask her to go round to their houses and, if she liked them, she would. In this instance, the man she was seeing regularly loitered around an area called Bonn Square. He was Eastern European and would hang out with a group of men who spent their days in that particular part of town, drinking and attempting to pick up young girls.

As we walked through the square, he saw her and called us over.

'Let's go to mine.'

He had a car and his house was on the way to my house so it would just be like getting a lift home, I reasoned. We agreed, walked to where his car was parked and he drove us the short distance back to his house. There were two other men in the car with us. I didn't know who they were but had seen them hanging around the house; there seemed to be quite a few single men who lived there. They didn't speak to me but chatted and laughed among themselves in a language I didn't understand.

We got to the house, followed the men inside and sat for a while chatting. I felt uneasy and sat with Jennifer. After a while, she got up and disappeared into another room with the man she knew and left me in the lounge with the two men from the car. One was greasy-looking. He had thick, black, wavy hair and a rough, unshaven face; he was also stocky. His friend was huge, over 6ft tall. I felt awkward and uncomfortable – they were looking at me menacingly. I went and sat on the sofa and they sat on either side of me. Then they grabbed me. I started screaming and struggling; I called to Jennifer for help but she didn't answer. One of the men pinned me down. They were talking to each other incomprehensibly. One started pulling at my clothes. Petrified, I screamed again.

Jennifer called out from the other room.

'I'll be there in a minute.'

While one of the men held me down, the other one raped me. I struggled and cried and begged them to stop but they just laughed. When he'd finished, he patted me on the head. I pulled my clothes together and ran out of the house. The thoughts inside my head were deafening. It's OK, I told myself, it's over now; it's happened before, it's no big deal. I took deep breaths and tried to stop myself from shaking. More than anything, I felt angry that I had let it happen – I thought it was my fault. After all, I'd entered the house willingly.

There was a garage next door to the house and I went in there, bought cigarettes and pretended nothing had happened. As I hurried home, I breathed deeply, fighting the panic inside. I ran a bath as soon as I got in and tried to wash the self-loathing away. It felt like I would never be clean again. I knew I wasn't going to report it because I was scared what people would think of me and what might happen: previously I had never been taken seriously so why would anyone believe me now?

As the weeks passed, I tried to forget what had happened. I told Jennifer and she attempted to brush it under the carpet. Each time I passed the house where it happened I felt a surge of panic. I became quiet and withdrawn. Mum noticed the change in me. We had to drive past their house all the time and I was fed up with seeing it. Each time it reminded me and I was finding it hard to hold things in. I needed someone to know what had happened and there was no one better than Mum. She was always very good at watching the signs, dropping questions in the conversation at the right time and she could tell something was wrong. I knew I could trust her and one day, around a month after the rape, we drove past the house again and she asked if something had happened that I wanted to talk about. I started talking.

'I've been raped,' I said.

Mum tried to remain calm and began asking general questions until she got a picture of what had happened.

'We have to report this to the police,' she told me.

I nodded. She turned the car round, drove me home and called the Oxford Constabulary. They came to the house and then asked me to make a statement. Then they asked if they could do a medical examination on me but I refused – I didn't want anyone to touch me and I couldn't see the point as I assumed it would have been too late to collect any evidence. I was taken to a special house, where rape victims go to be examined and I was interviewed by officers trained in speaking to victims of sexual assault. The house was less formal than a police station and set out like a normal, comfortable home with sofas, a kitchen and a bathroom. My interview was recorded – the microphone was hidden in a potted plant so I felt more relaxed. The police subsequently contacted Jennifer and her mother, and they raided the house where the assault happened and arrested the men. They remanded three in custody but eventually let them go and charged one, the man who raped me. I was asked to attend an ID parade, which I did, and then I didn't hear anything for ages.

Weeks later, Mum got a letter out of the blue from the Crown Prosecution Service. It stated that they could not proceed with the case. She rang to find out why and was told that, although my evidence was clear and consistent and the police believed me, unfortunately Jennifer's evidence was inconsistent, had changed and contradicted mine on several key points. They felt they would not be able to get a conviction as Jennifer would have been a crucial witness and there was no DNA evidence.

I wasn't shocked or surprised when the case didn't go ahead. The past had taught me that a child's word was never believed over that of an adult; the collapse of the case reinforced my view that it was better to keep quiet. For those reasons I didn't even hold it against Jennifer. Even if she had been consistent in what she said, I doubted a jury would have believed me.

After the case fell apart I would see the man around Oxford, trying to pick up other young girls. Once Mum saw him with a group of young girls and called the police. She stayed with the girls until they arrived. But it didn't put the gang off – they were very visible, they didn't care; they would pluck a child in front of you.

Several years later, Mum and I were discussing the incident and she reminded me of part of the statement I had given. I was asked to describe the room where the rape took place. I explained that I had been sitting on a chair with Jennifer before the attack. I was sitting on her knee, sucking my thumb. Scared and childlike, yet still the monster raped me.

For the months after that I didn't see much of Jennifer. My confidence was low, I wasn't at school, and I was aimless and listless. I became bored easily.

One afternoon I was out with a couple of friends, Sam and Justine – I knew them from school and they were nice girls. I was about to go and babysit for a friend of the family. We were walking over a bridge near home when a man approached us.

'All right, girls, do you want to go for a drink?' he asked.

None of us had seen him before; he came out of nowhere and was totally brazen. The others ignored him. One muttered the word 'sleazebag' under her breath. So, instead, he addressed me.

'What do you reckon, then?' he said, blanking Sam and Justine.

He locked on to me – perhaps he could see something about the way I looked that singled me out as an easy victim.

I was flattered by the attention – he seemed nice. Dark-skinned, he looked Arabic. Tall, with a thin face, goatee beard, brown teeth and big, bulging eyes, he looked to be in his mid-twenties. I thought it was cool that he was talking to me; he seemed friendly. He wore a big puffer jacket, jeans and a hat with flaps hanging over his ears.

It was freezing cold and the other girls were telling me to ignore him and move on.

'I can't go now, I'm babysitting,' I told him.

'What about another day? I'll take you to The Swan in Cowley,' he said. Cowley was a rough part of Oxford – the population was mostly Pakistani, Arabic and Muslim. The thought of going to a pub with an older man excited me.

'Give me your number,' he said. 'I'll call you.'

I told him my number and he punched it into his phone.

'My name is Mohammed, by the way,' he said, before he sloped off.

Sam tutted.

'Do you realise how much older than you he is?' she said disapprovingly.

But I didn't care.

That was the day my life changed in a way I could never have imagined.

Chapter ten

EGYPTIAN MO

Later that evening Sam tried to warn me again. She was older and wiser than me and knew exactly the kind of person Mohammed was, and what he was after. She was streetwise and smart; I thought I was too but, in reality, I was easily led and inexperienced.

'You shouldn't even make eye contact with people like that, let alone talk to them,' she told me.

But I had been chatty, friendly and open and Mohammed Karrar picked up on all the cues. A young girl in the cold, wearing skimpy clothes and make-up, I was more than ready to talk to strange older men and to hand over my phone number. He honed in on the vibes I was giving off and decided very quickly, through experience, that I was an easy target. I had 'victim' written all over me.

I had no idea that the random meeting was part of a plan and a process that he had gone through many times before with many different girls. He didn't want to speak to Sam or Justine because he knew just by looking at them and their body language that they wouldn't have any of it.

I ignored Sam's concerns. Surely he was just being friendly?

Initially Mohammed did all the chasing and at first I was flattered. I had low self-esteem and the confidence I showed outwardly masked a deep-seated insecurity. The truth was, I hated myself: I hid behind a façade of bravado and make-up. I would never look at myself in the mirror without make-up on. Instead, I would go to sleep with a full face on and wake with it still in place. Mum tried to get me to wear less but I didn't listen. I never took it off, I hid behind it.

It felt grown up to have the attentions of an older man. He sent me a text the following day.

'R U still on for that drink?'

I played it cool at first and didn't answer for a while. He persisted and his text messages continued. Each one asked me where I was and when he could meet me. After a few days of texting back and forth, I realised he didn't have a job. He texted every day and each time told me he was free if I wanted to meet him. I wondered what kind of grown-up didn't have a job, all of Mum's friends did. But then again before I met Mum I was passed through a succession of jobless adults so it didn't bother me.

For several days I kept avoiding the issue and wouldn't commit, then I tired of his persistence and decided to meet him. I wasn't at school at the time and he must have known this because, whenever he texted and asked what I was doing, usually I told him I was out with friends or at home watching TV. He knew that a child my age who wasn't at school would have certain issues and probably led a disrupted life. If I wasn't hanging out with my truanting friends, my days were mapped out with *Jeremy Kyle* and Facebook. I grew bored easily and was looking for something to do – another reason I was easy prey.

'OK,' I texted, 'where shall we meet?'

At first our meeting had been sold to me like a date: we were going to go out for a drink. The prospect excited me. It was something to punctuate the boredom and I had never been on a date before. I had never had a normal relationship, gone to the cinema, let alone gone for a walk in the park with a boy. He told me we were going to have a drink and get to know each other.

Then he told me to meet him at a flat in Riverside Court, a rundown block of flats near to my home. He asked what I liked to drink and what I smoked. I told him Stella, WKD, Irn-Bru and Superkings. It didn't sound like the date he had been describing, but it was a gloomy afternoon and so I agreed anyway. He texted me the number of the flat he was in and told me to meet him there in an hour. I pulled on a tight pair of jeans, with angel wings embossed across the back pocket, and a pair of pink suede boots. Then I reapplied my make-up, flicked on some eyeliner and told Mum I was going to see a friend. I knew it wasn't right, but I was nonetheless excited.

Riverside Court was a collection of flats originally built by Oxford City Council for those with special needs. It was full of people with learning disabilities, drug problems and mental health issues. A lot of very vulnerable people were placed there initially and then, over the years, the council started putting families there as well. It was well known as a problem estate. There were over 70 flats, occupied by a combination of very vulnerable people, families and drug dealers. This was where Mohammed told me he lived. To get there I walked along the river towpath and, when I got to the block he was in, I texted to tell him I was outside. He buzzed me in and was waiting by the door for me.

We said hello and I felt awkward as he ushered me inside. The studio flat was very smoky but the smoke smelled strange, like burned plastic. I walked into the white haze and it caught in the back of my throat. Mohammed laughed. I didn't know it at the time but the flat was a crack den. Unlike cigarette smoke, if you smoke crack in an enclosed space the fumes do not dissipate; they stay there, hanging in the air. Mohammed was wired when I walked in; energetic and talkative. There was no sign of the drugs he had been taking, but the flat was filthy. The carpet was heavily stained and sticky to tread on. There was a blue sofa covered in stains and a TV. It looked as if it hadn't been cleaned for ages and it didn't feel like a home. There were hardly any furnishings; it was sparse and claustrophobic. It didn't seem to matter at the time, though. Mohammed seemed really friendly and welcoming. He asked me about myself, where I lived, who I lived with, what I did. He never asked my age. He was on his own, but he told me a couple of his friends were coming over.

'You'll like them,' he said. 'They're good guys.'

A little while later two men arrived. They all talked in street slang and had gang names – Mohammed was 'Egyptian

Mo'. He wasn't from Egypt, but he looked like he could have been. I found out later that he was from a country called Eritrea.

The other men had brought different drinks with them, including the Stella, WKD and Superkings I had requested. I thought it was a lovely gesture and we sat around drinking and watching music channels on the TV. There was no food. When I started to look around the flat, I realised there was nothing in any of the cupboards. It was as if no one lived there.

The more I drank, the more I relaxed. And, as I did so, Mohammed continued to ask questions. He was very clever – he was finding out where I came from, whether I was adopted, whether my father was in my life, whether I had brothers and sisters, what I liked and didn't like. He didn't really encourage me to drink, he just let it be known that it was there if I wanted it and that I should help myself; he gave me the rope to hang myself. I kept drinking because the more I drank, the more comfortable I felt. He asked specifically about Mum. What annoyed me about her, and what we argued over.

I know now that he was trying to find out as many details about me as possible to assess whether I was suitable for what he and his cronies had in mind. He was storing information so he could use it. He knew exactly what he was doing; without a doubt he'd done it before.

When I started to open up about my background he leaned forward and touched my arm; he frowned in mock concern and pretended to get emotional. He was a good actor – he could make his eyes well up while listening to my stories.

And I believed that he cared. I was drunk, and he had me: it only took someone to pretend to understand me and to care and I was hooked in. In all, I was there a couple of hours the first time we met. He didn't encourage me to stay and he didn't press for anything physical. When I told him I had to go, he didn't try to stop me and he didn't tell me not to tell Mum about our meeting – he knew I wouldn't.

'OK, nice to meet you,' he said.

In a way I felt relieved to get out. While his concern was flattering, I found it exhausting to be talking about myself for so long – I wasn't used to people showing that level of interest in me. As I walked home and started to sober up, I wondered whether we had been talking or if he had been interrogating me. I realised I knew nothing about him – he didn't offer any information and I didn't feel I was invited to ask. Still, I thought I had met a nice guy. Tired and drunk, I was more concerned about what Mum would think because she would be able to tell I had been drinking.

When I got home I had to knock on the door because I had no key. Mum didn't let me have one. It was the best way she knew to keep a check on me and to try to control when I was coming and going. When Mum answered, she asked where I had been and who I had been with.

'Friends,' I shot back. I made it plain there was no discussion to have.

'What kind of friends?' she asked. 'The type that buy you alcohol?'

Pushing past her, I went straight to my room.

Mohammed texted me later to make sure I got home. Over the following days, he continued to text. 'Where are you?', 'What are you doing?', 'Do you fancy meeting up?'… Although the tone was insistent, I was pleased that he was so keen to see me again. I thought perhaps he was a bit desperate but I was being chased and I liked it – I hadn't had that sort of attention from a man before. On average he would send around four text messages a day. Sometimes he would ask who I was with.

A few days after our first meeting we arranged to meet again. It was the same pattern as before. He asked me to go to the flat in Riverside Court, and when I got there we smoked cigarettes and he provided alcohol for me. He was friendly, he was tactile, but he never overstepped the mark. Meanwhile, he continued to delve into my life and my past. He asked questions about my dating history and the men I knew.

'Make sure you text me back,' he said when I left. Within 30 minutes my phone was beeping: 'Are you home?', 'Who are you with?' He was controlling me from the start but I didn't realise this.

The contact continued and a few weeks after our first meeting I started to feel nervous. By now the attention was overwhelming and, although he had never done anything to make me feel threatened, I worried that I had given too much away and that he seemed overly eager. But I told myself he was my friend and, when he failed to go away, I texted him back and saw him again. It was becoming a regular thing and there was a part of me that was excited about going to the flat.

While my relationship with Mohammed established itself, life at home became increasingly fraught. I was arguing with Mum and she knew something was afoot. She registered that I was constantly on my phone and that I was going out and drinking.

I was still seeing Terri and my brothers and sister three times a year. Terri was pregnant again – didn't know who the father was. On one visit, during her pregnancy, she had clearly been drinking. It repulsed me and made me angry to see her neglect yet another child. I just wasn't interested in her anymore, and it saddened me to realise that I had less and less in common with my siblings. We had all started to move on and our lives were heading in different directions. I wasn't interested in running around in Wacky Warehouse anymore. Conversations became forced and awkward. The meetings were still held in kids' places and my brothers never grew up – they would play fight all the time. It was easier for them to see each other because they would just roll around on the floor and play, whereas Kirsten and I would struggle to find things to talk to them about.

I told Mohammed about the meetings and he nodded and pretended to understand. I was spending longer and longer with him. At first I only saw him in the afternoon and stayed for a couple of hours. Then it extended until after dark, then into the night and the early hours of the morning. Mum called and texted to find out where I was and waited up to question me when I got back. I didn't tell her anything and just shouted when she asked who I had been with.

Mohammed and I never went out. It became clear early on, when he realised I could trust him, that he was a drug dealer. He was very open about it and he explained to me about the different drugs: crack, heroin and cocaine. He made them sound harmless and exciting.

'Would you try drugs?' he asked.

'I might try crack,' I answered, 'but I would never do heroin.'

'What about cocaine? It's much weaker than crack.'

'Yeah, I'd do that,' I said. And with that, he pulled a wrap of cocaine from his pocket, cut up two lines on the coffee table, snorted one and offered me the rolled-up £10 note he'd used. I took it and snorted my first line of cocaine without really thinking. If he said it was weak, it must be. My nose went numb. I hated the sensation – it left a bitter taste at the back of my throat. After a few minutes, I felt light-headed and I started to relax but felt alert. It was a good feeling.

I began to work out that the flat wasn't Mohammed's home. There was another man who was there most of the time, Steve. He was a creep and disgusting, and it appeared that he lived there.

We talked about what I had done in the time I had not been with Mohammed and I thought it was nice because he seemed to want to get to know my mum. He asked all about her, what she worked as, how old she was, whether she had family, and he asked about my adoption and the other carers I had lived with too. Very quickly he found out there were no male figures in my life. He focused on my home life and didn't want to know about extended family; he wanted to know whether there was a father figure or someone protective. He asked about my elder brother and where he lived. When he found out that Jayden lived in Cheshire, he seemed relieved. He asked how close we were and how often I saw him. With hindsight, if I'd said I have a dad at home who is 6ft and has a history of violence or told him my dad was a policeman, things may have turned out very differently.

Soon I was sucked in, deeper and deeper. If I had a bad day, I went straight to the flat to talk about my problems. Mohammed listened intently and continued to supply booze, cocaine and cigarettes and to tell me about drugs. He started to openly take them in front of me. I ended up there every day – I told him what was wrong and what had happened and he fixed it with booze and cocaine. There were no alarm bells – I thought he cared about me, I thought he was my friend.

He seemed to understand my life better than anyone and he started the process of twisting my thoughts and feelings. Slowly, and in a very calculated way, he began to turn me against my mum. She in turn became increasingly suspicious the more I disappeared. I always came back drunk and she saw a pattern developing. My phone rang or I got a text message and soon after I left the house. She asked where I was going and I started an argument. Sometimes I found a reason to start an argument before she even asked just so I had an excuse to storm out of the house. She had a good idea that I was seeing a man but, whenever she asked, I lied and said I was with friends.

Mohammed told me she was jealous that I was having a relationship. He said that she would try her best to stop me going out, and she did. I thought he was incredibly sensitive, he understood me and knew everything. He wasn't a genius, though: Mum was just doing what any good parent would.

When I was with him I drank and the more I drank, the more I opened up. I told him about the abuse and neglect when I was little; about the rape. He pretended to well up and tried to make himself cry. Then he started stroking my leg. He gained my trust and encouraged me to confide in him and the more I did, the more power he had over me. After weeks of these meetings, I still knew nothing about him: he never gave anything back. I never felt I was in a relationship with him. I went there because it was somewhere to go and he showed me attention and provided me with drink, drugs and cigarettes.

I never saw him drive a car. If he needed to go out, people picked him up and took him places or he got taxis. People came and went, and passed through the flat. Some stayed, smoked crack and leered at me. Many of them seemed to be related to Mohammed or part of a gang, and the longer I knew Mohammed, the more I got to know them.

A few months after I first met him, I was out with a friend in a park near home. I had been drinking and I was wearing a skimpy top and jeans. It was a cold day and, as we chatted, a huge guy I recognised from the flat called out my name and came over to us. He was wearing a long, heavy leather coat and he took it off and put it over my shoulders.

'You're going to freeze dressed like that,' he told me. 'I'll give you a lift home.'

I had only seen him a few times before. His name was Akhtar Dogar, but I knew him by his gang name: 'Spider'. He was a tough-looking man with a wide, aggressive face and on the few occasions I'd seen him at the flat he had been with his brother, Anjum, who was known as 'Jammy'. At the time I thought nothing of it and just assumed he was being friendly so I followed him to his car and got in, despite my friend telling me not to. I didn't even think there was anything strange about the fact that he knew my name and what road I lived on. I directed him to my house and he dropped me off outside. From that point on, he knew my full address.

Both Mohammed and Spider were part of a gang of criminals; they had different territories they controlled and dealt drugs in. Spider ran the Cowley area, where the main road was lined with Halal shops, kebab shops, chicken huts and bookmakers. There were perverts everywhere. Walking through Cowley, I would regularly be accosted. I went there because one of the convenience stores served me alcohol. There were a lot of men loitering on the streets and I learned that they were usually drug dealers and, although there were normal families living in the area, the streets around Cowley were full of drug dens. These were marked out by signs: if there was a pair of trainers thrown over the telephone wire leading into a property, this indicated there were drugs available inside. The dealers left the lids of the salt bins open on the corners of the streets where they lived to signify that they had stuff to sell, but most of the time they just shouted down the street. They weren't scared, they ran the place. Spider seemed to be the main player, the one they answered to, even though there were two territories. Fearsome, he didn't have to do anything threatening – you just knew from the way he looked that he was evil.

I learned about the drug trade from Mohammed but what I didn't know was that he had been speaking to Spider about me and a project he was working on. They had other business interests – young girls – and I was part of their plan.

I was drinking increasing amounts of alcohol, all supplied by Mohammed. At first I drank because I thought it was cool and after that I carried on to block out everything else that happened. In the beginning, I was enjoying alcohol and the more I drank, the more I seemed to be sucked into the underworld of the city. I was starting to see the dark underbelly of Oxford. There was a life and community below the surface hugely at odds with the image the city has; it was also hugely at odds with the household I had been adopted into. It was full of seedy, menacing characters; also victims, junkies and runaway, vulnerable children.

There was a prevalent underage drinking culture in the city and, through it, I met a whole new group of friends. It centred on Bonn Square, where a gang of kids used to meet, loiter and get drunk. I had a head start on this scene because I was always given alcohol by Mohammed, and Oxford lends itself to drinking because it's a student town and there are a lot of pubs and bars – there were drunk people around all the time.

My friends then included Dean, Joey and Kasey, who were part of a gang of feral children who hung around the city. None of them was schooled and they practically lived on the streets and largely didn't care. Kasey's parents were deaf and had learning difficulties. Dean was a street kid – his mum had died when he was young and he lived with his dad. Joey was disturbed. He once threw a brick through a residential window and almost killed a baby sleeping inside. Mum's house was fairly central and I would see these kids hanging around outside; they also hung out in a sink estate called Friars Wharf and an area known as Thames Street. Mum once took two of them home when she caught them running wild in the street and breaking windows.

I spent a lot of time with Kasey. We met when she asked me for a cigarette at a fair in the city. She was a couple of years younger than me and tall and skinny. At 12 she looked 16 but mentally she was very young. She looked like she was on drugs. Kasey had red hair and pale grey skin; her cheeks were sunken and there were dark shadows under her eyes. She was wild – her moods swung up down. She was like a fizzing bottle of cola. Always cheeky and a bit rude to adults, she had had a very hard life. Her mother and father had a range of health issues and so she had to grow up fast. Kasey was wild but there was something vulnerable about her too. She wouldn't open up readily and talk about her life and, like me, she seemed stuck in a self-destructive pattern.

This surreal other world was like a layer beneath normal life. Soon I was able to spot the people who lived there in the same way experience had taught me how to pick out a child in care: the people in this world had a look of loneliness and empty eyes.

Now I had two lives. I had my normal friends who went to school. Always having a go at me and telling me to sort myself out and get back into school, they loved and respected my mum and could see what a good person she was. They sat with her when I disappeared to Mohammed's, and they texted me to tell me to come back because Mum was worried sick.

The months passed and Mohammed strengthened his links with me. Always he reminded me what a good friend he was, and how much he knew about me. On a few occasions, when I was very drunk, he touched me. Once, when I was paralytic, he persuaded me to perform a sex act on him, but we were never in a relationship. Increasingly, he talked about sexual subjects and made sexual remarks: he would tell me what he wanted to do to me, he would say he had done this with other people. I just thought he was being a lad. He told me I could always trust him.

There were always drugs around and I became increasingly nonchalant about them. Mohammed supplied me with cocaine and on one occasion he made a joint for me. I smoked it, but it made me feel ill. Also, he continually talked about crack – it was like he was a salesman. He exposed me to it daily and got me used to seeing it around, to the distinct smell of it and the sight of people smoking it. For me it had lost its shock value and, once it did, he started to get me curious about it. He told me how good it felt and that it was no big deal – he and his friends smoked it so regularly it was like they were smoking cigarettes. I started to get interested in trying it but was still apprehensive. On a few occasions, he asked outright whether I wanted some and I said no.

Subtle pressure was being placed on me. Everything was building up to getting me to try it, but in such a way that I wouldn't be scared off. Finally, I gave in. One Friday, Mohammed told me we were going to have a weekend session.

'We are going to have a drink session and a party,' he stated. 'It will be a late one.'

I took this to mean that it was planned to be an all-nighter.

'Why don't you try some crack? It'll keep you awake.'

'OK,' I nodded.

The next evening I went to the flat as usual after running away from home. I knew Mum was worried sick about my constant disappearances, and she regularly called the police when I went, but I didn't care. Like Mohammed said, she was the enemy: she was jealous because I was having a good time.

He was there with two other men.

'Remember you said last time that you will try it,' he reminded me as he tapped some crystals from a plastic bag.

I was nervous but there was pressure on me to do it, and I wasn't one for stepping down from a dare.

He handed me a small glass pipe. At one end was a funnel-shaped opening in which he placed a crack rock. I lit a lighter and held it over the rock as I inhaled the acrid smoke that filled the tube – I had seen him and the others do so a hundred times so he didn't have to tell me what to do. I held the pipe and lit the flame but it might as well have been his hands on it because it was his work and persistence over the months that had got me into a position where I was willing to try hard drugs for him: I was 13.

The feeling was instant. A wave of tingly euphoria swept over me and all my cares evaporated; I felt great and happy.

I looked up and Mohammed and the other men were watching and grinning. When the hit wore off after a few minutes I craved another and Mohammed delivered. The music sounded better, everything looked and felt better.

I didn't immediately notice the change in the atmosphere of the room. I didn't think much of it when Mohammed said that I was his bitch and later called me a ho. I was high and, as long as he kept satisfying my cravings, I didn't care what he said. He started talking about sex and about what I would do for him; I didn't understand what he meant. Lost in a haze, I was grinning and nodding at the words as the faces around me swam in and out of focus.

'Next time you come round there will be a couple of lads here. You are going to do me a favour, aren't you?' he whispered as my eyes rolled in my head.

That night I took lots of drugs and felt shaky when he sent me home. I cried myself to sleep – I thought I was addicted and then I got scared about what was going to happen to me. Before I met Mohammed I had hated drugs – I thought they were disgusting. I saw people in the city who were obviously on them, and I didn't want to be like them: zombies, empty shells. That day I was vile to Mum. I argued and sulked and, when she asked where I had been, I spat back that it was nothing to do with her and I had been with friends.

As the fog in my head cleared, I tried hard to fight the cravings but I really wanted more. I told myself it was a one-off but I knew it wouldn't be – it felt so good and it was so easily available. I could see why people got addicted. And I had a nagging fear: Mohammed wanted me to do something for him and I had agreed. He knew so much about me. I could trust him, couldn't I? I was too scared to say no because he could give me drugs and make me feel so good. I tried to work out what was happening. Why was I so worried about how Mohammed was acting? What did he want me to do?

Somewhere in the dark recesses of my mind I knew and the thought terrified me so I shut it away. He told me I owed him because I was smoking his drugs but he didn't want money from me. Instead, he wanted a favour from me: I owed him because of all he'd done for me since I'd met him. I was confused about it all but the overriding feeling was that I wanted to take more drugs – and I wanted to please Mohammed.

Nothing else mattered.

Chapter eleven
PAYBACK

When I got up the following day, I had a bath and put my phone on loud because Mum was at work and I was scared of missing the call I knew was coming. I was supposed to go to anger management classes, which had been booked for me through social services. It was part of the effort everyone was making to get me to address my behaviour, so I could get to a place where I was able to go back to school. But I had no intention of going back.

As I got myself ready, I looked in the mirror. The girl staring back at me was pale and thin; I was anxious and I felt sick. I hadn't been eating properly over the previous months, due to the amount I was drinking and the drugs I was taking. Usually I vomited if I ate. Whenever I came home, Mum always tried to make me eat but I wasn't hungry. She knew I was drinking and she probably suspected I was taking drugs. She was worried sick and tried again and again to speak to me, and discover what was happening and how she could help, but I shut her out.

I went downstairs and got myself a glass of water but it came back up seconds after I drank it. Scared and nervous, I felt cornered. I worried that if I didn't go and do what Mohammed was going to ask me then he would come to my house and get me anyway. When my phone buzzed, I jumped. I grabbed it quickly and read the message.

'Make sure you are here on time, my friends will be waiting,' he texted.

My hands were shaking as I read it.

It was easy leaving the house because Mum was at work – at least I didn't have to argue my way out the front door or climb out the window. I got to the flat early. When I arrived, Mohammed's whole demeanour had changed. He talked down to me and he ordered me around; he was hostile and I didn't like it. He gave me drink and then he smoked a crack pipe. When I smelled the acrid smoke, I started to shiver. He looked at me, smiled and offered me the pipe. I inhaled. All my senses cleared.

Mohammed reminded me how much I'd smoked the night before. It was around £100 worth, about four rocks. He made it plain that I owed him for it and that, to repay him, I was to have sex with the men he was about to introduce me to. That was the way it worked. If I wanted to enjoy the drink and the drugs, and be part of his life, I had to do things for him. Ever since that day, I have struggled to understand why I didn't just walk away at that point. Why didn't I call the police or tell my mum? And for years afterwards I blamed myself. I thought it was all my fault, but I had been brainwashed. It had taken months of careful grooming to get me to the point where I was unable to make rational decisions for myself. I had been targeted and manipulated. Mohammed knew exactly the kind of girl I was; he knew I came from a disruptive background, that I was vulnerable and easily led. He knew that, because I was sexually abused when I was young, I was averse to physical relationships so he didn't try to be my boyfriend, instead he positioned himself as a trusted friend. If I had been a different girl, he would have used different tactics: he would have positioned himself as a long-term partner and spoilt me with gifts and promises of love. I later learned that he did just that with one of the other girls he controlled; his methods depended on the history of the target.

The psychological work done, he started with drink and then progressed to drugs until I was reliant on him. And then he switched from trusted friend to malevolent master. There was a threat in the way he ordered me around; he was in complete control. And so I did what he told me to do. He made it plain what was expected of me. And I knew it was coming. I was already a mess, already on drugs and crack was the next stage; I was in thrall to the way it made me feel and it also served to numb me against what was going to happen. I told myself I could get through it.

The drugs made me unaware of the environment I was in; I didn't feel in any danger. I convinced myself I wasn't in a crack den; I shut out thoughts about what I was about to do. Now I was his – I was a piece of meat. Through the crack buzz he told me what I was going to do: his friends would arrive and I would have sex with them.

'You are mine now,' he sneered.

He led me into a room where there was a bed, on which he'd placed a carrier bag.

'Get that lot on!' he ordered me.

Inside was a range of underwear. All adult and highly sexualised, with stockings and a corset, it left nothing to the imagination. Obviously, given my young age, I'd never worn anything like it.

I challenged him at that point and told him I didn't want to do it. That's when he made the first threat.

'Do as I say, bitch, or you'll get a smack!' he said, raising his hand to me and I cowered.

I knew I had no choice. Had I refused, he would force me into the clothes, or worse. I knew he was capable of violence and was left in no doubt that he would hit me. In the past he had spoken freely about hitting women. He once talked about an ex of his, explaining she got 'chopsy' and that he gave her a slap to sort her out. I didn't know what 'chopsy' meant but it didn't matter; he had no moral hang-ups about beating women. It was a side of him I didn't like and it made me feel uncomfortable at the time. But I thought he was my friend and I assumed he would never do anything to hurt me. I owed him, and the underwear and what went with it was part of the deal. So I took off my jeans, sweater and underwear, and did what he told me. I'd never worn a corset and it was fiddly trying to get it on correctly; I felt embarrassed and exposed.

Once I'd put on the clothes, he switched back to being nice to me – he was making sure I knew what the boundaries were.

'You look good,' he leered.

He pulled out his crack pipe and offered me a hit. I took it – I knew it would help me with what was to come.

Then he held up his phone and started taking photos of me. I didn't know why he did this at the time, but later I realised that he would text out those pictures to customers to advertise me.

I was a girl for sale.

A short while later, two men came round. I was given more crack and told to sit on the sofa while Mohammed talked to them briefly and took money from them. They had sex with me. I shut it all out – I did what I was told to do and didn't look them in the eye. Mohammed stood in the background, watching. They didn't even bother to undress, they just pulled their trousers down.

When they'd finished, they said goodbye to Mohammed and left.

'Change now,' he sniffed. 'Leave the clothes here.'

I was in shock and traumatised. In my mind, I was trying to justify what I'd just done and attempting to come to terms with it. Before I left he told me to come back the following day as there was another job. That's how he described it – as work.

Back home I ran a steaming bath. The water was scalding when I stepped in but the pain felt good. I wanted to bleach myself and remove any trace of the men. I scrubbed myself hard until my skin was red. Mum had cooked food and I asked her to cut it up into tiny pieces and feed me – I wanted to be a child again. I sat on her lap and asked her to stroke my hair. I knew now that I had crossed a line. I was scared about what I'd done and what had been taken from me. I belonged to Mohammed, but I wanted to be a little girl again – I wanted a second chance at childhood.

It happened again the next day, and the day after that. Each time I pushed against the waves of panic that threatened to swamp me. And it got easier. I drank, I was given drugs and I went off into a place in my mind where no one could touch me. It was different men each time. Sometimes the men wanted to have a drink first and a chat. I ignored them and Mohammed would tell me menacingly to be nice. It always happened in the same place.

Around the third or fourth time I discovered some men were violent. The 'customer' that day started to choke me. He was doing it for his own gratification and, as he squeezed my neck, I panicked and lashed out at him. He hit me back and swore at me. I was frightened but Mohammed did nothing. I was crying and refused to comply with the man's wishes so he walked over and produced his crack pipe to ease me. Like a baby, I was suckling for comfort. I inhaled the smoke and relaxed. He was medicating me, I was being anaesthetised but I wouldn't have got through it any other way.

Mohammed knew just what dosage to give me. He balanced the drink out with the drugs, knowing the more drunk I was, the more incapable and compliant I would be; he used the crack to keep me lucid because crack takes the dullness off being drunk. Whenever I'd start to waiver or looked as if I wasn't going to do what I was told he would give me crack. It made my head feel like it was exploding in a burst of rapture and I would suddenly smile. The feeling was fleeting but lasted long enough to get me through the moments of deep doubt and fear. Away from the source of the drugs, I was anxious and jittery. All I could think of was how to get more: drugs and drink wiped the slate clean.

After the man hit me and had left, I shouted at Mohammed. 'Why did you let him do that?'

I slapped him because I blamed him. He was there and he saw me being choked, but did nothing to protect me. In return, he punched me in the face with a clenched fist. But it didn't shock me – I held my face and glared at him.

When I got home as usual Mum tried to find out where I had been. She noticed that my face was swollen and asked what had happened so I told her I had had a fight with a girl. But I wasn't going to tell her a thing. I didn't respect her – I was always fearful of adults until I met Mum and then I realised she wasn't violent, so I assumed I could get away with anything. She wasn't ever going to hurt me and I took advantage of that.

I was determined to keep pushing and pushing her. I am not a nasty person but I became nasty to her. On the occasions when we were getting along, I would look for ways to upset her. I stole money from her – I took her debit card after memorising her PIN. I wanted to get money out to try to pay Mohammed back for the drugs I was using in the hope that I could stop myself from being sold. But it didn't work: he refused the cash and I was arrested for theft: Mum reported me because she wanted me to learn a lesson. But I didn't care what she or the police said. She would always call the police when I went missing and they contacted social services. Everyone was involved and she was desperate. She tried to get help but social services treated her as a nuisance. Over the years there were over 80 reports of me missing and in the end she was told to stop reporting me until I had been gone for more than 24 hours.

Mum was at the end of her tether; she knew something was happening and she had her suspicions that I was disappearing to see an older man, but in those early days she did not know the full extent. She was careful never to challenge me when I was upset because I tended to go wild and, although I always bottled up my emotions, when I returned home from being prostituted, I did get emotional. I was scared and ashamed.

After Mohammed had broken me down, got me hooked on drugs and turned me to prostitution I was reintroduced to Spider, the man I had met in the park almost a year ago. I was told that I also had to work for him. Spider knew Mohammed had been grooming me; he monitored my progress. Sometimes he turned up outside the flat in his car and Mohammed went down to speak to him.

There was no choice but to do as Spider told me: he had a fearsome reputation and he also knew where I lived. He wasn't worried about the police and I was terrified that he would turn up at my house and tell Mum what I'd done.

After I had finished at Riverside Court, I was sent across town to Cowley Road, where Spider and Jammy would have men waiting for me. Although they were rivals in the drug trade, they put their differences aside and worked together when the business was girls.

I was petrified of Spider. When I was with him I became scared and timid; I was his slave and he ran a modern-day slave trade.

Each day there would be a man to go with, usually more than one. And the men running this industry were brazen. Mohammed thought nothing of calling my home number and wasn't at all concerned when my mum answered the phone. She would question him and he would abuse her and tell her to put me on the line; she would then tell him I was underage and threaten to call the police. She thought that maybe I was mixed up with an older man but didn't know the full extent of what was happening. There were occasions when she raised concerns with the police and social services, but because there was no proof of anything I wouldn't cooperate, and no action was taken. Mum was pulling her hair out and frantic with worry. I told her he was just a friend and that she was being paranoid. One day Spider turned up outside the house. He sat outside in his car. On seeing him, I panicked – I didn't want Mum to see because I didn't want her to know what I had been doing. I ran out and got in the vehicle and he drove off with me to meet a punter.

In the moments when my head was clear – which became less and less frequent due to the amount of drugs and drink

I was being fed – I wondered who I could turn to for advice. I was still in phone contact with Terri, my birth mother, and one day I confided in her about taking crack.

Any other mother who heard that from a daughter would be shocked. Terri was almost proud.

'Crack's fine,' she said dismissively. 'You can do that, it's not strong.'

I asked her how to stop taking it.

'It's fine, don't worry,' was all she could offer.

It felt like I was talking to another member of the gang. I didn't see her as family – I hadn't called her Mum since I was little. We never spoke like normal people.

The one person who could have saved me was the person I had been turned against. My feelings were so confused. I loved Mum and I cared about her. Part of me was devastated when I hurt her but still I continued to push her away, literally and metaphorically. I thought she was the enemy but I also knew she would be devastated and would do everything to help me if she knew the full extent of what was going on.

I was torn in two: I was Lara – the loving child, who wanted to be liked and did normal things and loved her family – and I was Lauren – a disturbed, drug-taking woman-child, who was exploited by sexual predators. It was a battle between the two and Lauren was winning.

Chapter twelve

LOST GIRL

The days were a haze of drugs, drink, danger and aimlessness. I woke around 10, moped about the house in my pyjamas and tried to forget what was happening to me. I smoked cigarettes and waited for my phone to ring. Mum knew I smoked by then and tried to discourage it. I had started around the time I was 12. I began just by experimenting, like a lot of children do when they get to secondary school, but I enjoyed it. I found that, when I was stressed or angry, a cigarette was the only thing that would calm me down. My smoking was the least of Mum's worries. She even bought me them sometimes, so at least she could control how much I smoked. If I didn't have any I begged them from strangers so she figured it was the safest option. She also knew they calmed me down when I got cross.

While I waited for the phone to ring I watched *Jeremy Kyle* and tried to convince myself that I wasn't the only person whose life was a mess.

When the call came, there was an odd sense of relief. I got anxious waiting because I knew what was coming. Once the call came through to tell me what time to be at the flat at least I wasn't waiting anymore; I got ready and went out. I knew he would call, he always did.

I spent my mornings with *Jeremy Kyle* and my afternoons, evenings and nights in a crack den. It was a vile place, no better than a squat, and it reminded me of the house I grew up in.

After Mohammed had found out all there was to know about me and coerced me to do his will, he hardly talked to me. I sat in the flat watching music channels while he fed me drugs and we waited for the punters to arrive.

Meanwhile, Mum was pulling her hair out, trying to coax me back into education. I may have been allowed back to school had I shown a willingness and, if not, the local education authority had a duty to provide me with some form of tutoring. I was given incentives all the time – shopping trips, horse riding, a pony, a puppy, a kitten. All I had to do was go to school, come in on time or do something that was good for me. But it was never enough. I'd ask for money as well; I pushed and pushed. I can't imagine what a shock it must have been for her to have me.

Mum adapted to my moods. She noticed my anger when I got home and waited until she could communicate with me. If I wasn't high on drugs, I was angry at what was happening to me. After the men, I went for walks before I returned home to try to clear my head because I was so cross with myself and with life. Mum tried so hard to find out what was happening and to find a way for us to get through it, but I clammed up or got aggressive.

If Mum was home when I got the call or text from Mohammed or Spider I engineered rows; I shouted at her and stormed out. If she tried to stop me, I pushed her out the way. I knew, if I didn't go to them, they would come and get me.

Their conversations with me were full of implied threats, not only against me but also against Mum and even Snowy.

'I know about that dog,' Mohammed would say. 'It would be such a shame if anything ever happened to it or your mum. She might fall over accidentally or get knocked down.'

Mum tried to alert anyone who would listen – the police, the local authority, politicians. No one seemed to know what to do. I had an outreach worker whom I saw regularly; we would go and do activities once a week; sometimes we would visit museums or I would go to lessons in a special unit. Social services assumed the problem lay at home and that the relationship between Mum and me was the issue. I learned much later that there was a suspicion I was prostituting or being prostituted, but because I was so obstructive whenever anyone asked, no one knew how to handle it.

Eventually action was taken, but it was taken on the basis that my home life was the problem. The assumption was that I was running *away* from something, rather than *to* something. In reality, on the rare days when I was left alone, Mum and I got on well and enjoyed each other's company. On the days when I wasn't required by Mohammed or Spider and Jammy – who I called 'the gang' – I didn't want to go anywhere, I was happy being at home. Still, the course of action that the authorities decided was best for me was to place me under a care order, effectively giving control of my life to social services, and to take me away from the perceived problem area – my home – and send me back into the care system.

It happened after I had gone missing overnight when it was decided that I must have run away because I didn't want to be with Mum, and so a place was found for me with a specialist foster carer for troubled children in the Southeast. I stayed there for a few weeks. It was uneventful and it changed nothing. When I returned to Oxford, I went missing a few days later. Mohammed knew I had returned and he texted me: there were more drugs and more men for me. I was wandering home in the morning, drunk and drugged, when I was spotted by a local police officer and taken to the station. Social services were called. I was questioned, became aggressive and refused to answer their questions. Again, it was decided the best course of action would be to temporarily remove me from my home and so I was transferred to a children's home in Cambridgeshire. I was taken there in a car by security guards. While Mum was glad something was being done, she was upset that I was being taken away and frustrated because she knew that the problem was not our relationship.

Although it was supposed to be a special home for children with behavioural issues, there was no security or boundaries; there didn't seem to be any rules. A big old house, the only residents were me and another girl. It was very fussy, the rooms were all perfect and clean and I didn't like it at all. When I first arrived there were pyjamas laid out on the bed but they weren't *my* pyjamas; it didn't feel comfortable. We were overseen by four members of staff. There was always an adult in residence, days were structured: there were formal lessons, free time and set mealtimes. For a while I played along with the routine but then I got bored and began to be disruptive after two weeks. I didn't get along with the other girl who was living there and we started to bicker and argue. She was troubled and so was I; we clashed over everything. Neither of us was trusting and I approached most new relationships and people in my life with suspicion. It was an enclosed environment, we weren't allowed out and as the days went on, I became increasingly frustrated.

As a prank one day I squirted her shampoo around the bathroom. She failed to see the funny side and we started an argument, which deteriorated into a fight. It was nasty and violent and the police were called. I was restrained and then taken away.

It was plain that I couldn't be returned to the home and so alternative accommodation was sought. I stayed in the police station for several hours after I had been charged with common assault and criminal damage, while social services were contacted and some unfortunate case worker back in Oxford rang round to find me somewhere suitable to stay. The answer they came up with was a similar residential home for disturbed children in Devon. I was never told whether that was the nearest placement or someone had assumed it would be better to send me almost as far away as it was geographically possible.

The arrangements took several hours to finalise and I was driven away in the early hours across the country to my new temporary home. Initially it was to be an eight-week placement. No one told Mum I had been sent to the West Country until the following day. I wasn't particularly bothered about where I was going, or what was going to happen to me when I got there; it was an adventure. It is hard to explain to people who have never been in the situation I was in but, apart from the anger that erupted in me regularly, I had no other feelings. I was numb.

The home was called Meadowside. We arrived in the morning and it was a scary, huge, imposing old building. To me, it looked like something from a horror movie. It was in the middle of nowhere, remote from any towns or villages. There was one other girl in there. Chrissy was around two years older than me and she was a mess: she had been taken to the home because, like me, she kept running away. She lived in Birmingham but was involved with a gang in London. She was being abused, and was also selling herself and being sold.

Although I was wary of her at first, we were both smokers and that broke the ice. On the first day I got there, she asked me if I was going for a fag and we both went outside and started talking. It was superficial stuff about the place and what went on inside it. I never spoke to her about why I was there and what was going on in my life – I never confided in anyone.

Chrissy told me she was leaving for a temporary visit to her mum later that day and asked if I would straighten her hair, which I did for her. In return, I asked to borrow some of her make-up.

'When I come back, we'll go out,' she winked.

I knew that meant escape.

The first night I was on my own and that gave me the creeps. The place was big and draughty; it creaked in the quiet and the area around was pitch-black. There was a communal room, with sofas, a television and a pile of board games but the kids who were sent there would not have been the type to sit down and play Monopoly.

There were two staff on hand throughout the night. I watched some TV and went to bed.

Later the following day Chrissy returned and told me to pack a small bag for the night – we would be going out. She explained that she knew someone in the nearby town who would be able to get us to London. After the boredom of the previous day and night, I was more than willing; I didn't want to be left there again on my own. I was ready to go when she knocked on my door after it got dark. It was Halloween night, which added to the sense of fun. The front door was locked and secured; it had a CCTV monitor over it. All the windows had heavy-duty locks on them, except for a small window in the bathroom, which we managed to jump through. We didn't even make much of an effort to hide what we were doing. The staff on duty that night noticed we had both gone in the bathroom together but didn't think anything of it until we were outside and running across the field opposite the house. When we got some distance away we stopped and crouched down to see what was happening. The security lights we triggered lit up the front and staff were scurrying around the grounds looking for us but they didn't look for long and went back inside after 10 minutes. We laughed and ran off into the night.

It was pitch-black, cold and scary but Chrissy knew where she was going. It took us over an hour trudging through fields and dimly lit country lanes before we came to the town. Chrissy led me to a small, rundown estate on the outskirts and to a grey, depressed-looking house. She rang the doorbell and a man answered.

He peered round the door and ushered us inside. He looked like a geek: pale and skinny, with long, lank, greasy hair. He wore an old sweater, stained combats and thick, plastic-rimmed glasses. When I saw him properly in the light of the hallway I actually laughed – he looked harmless. But when we followed him inside it immediately became apparent he wasn't. He led us to an upstairs room with blankets draped across the windows to hide what went on inside. It was set up like a photographic studio, with cameras on tripods. In the middle, there was a bed and strewn around were items of underwear. They were all ladies' garments and the same style that Mohammed had told me to wear: overtly sexual.

The man was part of a paedophile ring and I later learned had targeted the home because it was known as somewhere vulnerable children were sent. In paedophile parlance it was a 'honeypot', a place where predatory men could find pliable victims.

Of course now I know how shocking that is, but back then, in the midst of what I was going through with the gang in Oxford, it just seemed like a natural extension of my extreme life. Why wouldn't I find myself in a house with a runaway and a paedophile, plotting an escape to London? The man made it obvious what he wanted us to do: we were to meet his customers for sex. But first we had to disguise ourselves as he said the police would be looking for us. He kept hair dye in his bathroom and told us to use it. I dyed mine bright red and Chrissy streaked hers black and blonde. Then, just as Mohammed had done when he first started selling me, the man told us to put on the underwear and he took photos. Later, he gave us £500 in cash and told us to get to London. He directed us to a hotel in a place called Great Portland Street and told us to pay for the room in cash and wait there for the customers. Chrissy didn't question his instructions and neither did I; I followed blindly. I wanted to get away from the home and Chrissy had told me she knew where to get drugs when we got to the capital.

On the train journey we bought drink and no one questioned us when we booked into the hotel, which was clean, small and discreet. I was still just 13. We paid with the notes, as we had been told. Chrissy went off to meet some people she knew and it wasn't long before we had a supply of drugs.

The following days were a haze of drugs and drink. Men came to the hotel and abused us. Sometimes we were told by the abusers to go to other men. We travelled around London. When we were not being abused, we would hang around Camden, drinking and taking drugs with a gang of people Chrissy knew. At times I missed Mum, but I never missed Oxford. The fear of Mohammed and what would happen to me when I went back were always at the back of my mind. I never believed I could walk away from him.

Back in Oxford, Mum was distraught. She had been notified of my disappearance and was worried sick. It must have been awful for her. She was told that I could only be classed as a missing person, or 'misper' in police talk, once I had been gone longer than 24 hours. And so she waited until I had been gone long enough for the police to investigate, terrified the phone would ring or there would be a knock on the door and someone would be there to tell her I had been found dead. She was not stupid; she knew I was involved in some form of exploitation and was desperate to help me.

My disappearance to London was for much longer than 24 hours and, after Chrissy and I had been gone for several days, the police started to take the case seriously. There was a manhunt and an appeal on television news: as two vulnerable children there was concern for our safety. At one point, I was spotted in a place called Willesden on CCTV walking down a road and the investigation began to centre on London.

Meanwhile, Chrissy was introducing me to the people she knew around the city. Many of them were men. Looking back, it is obvious that she had been trafficked before, but at the time I didn't know what the term meant. We were being sold and the men using us must have been part of some form of network because often they would take us on to the next customer. We didn't travel with clothes, we were told to buy them when we got to London and we were told what clothes to buy: sexualised black lacy underwear and corsets.

At one point I was recognised by two police officers when I was walking down a street near the hotel we were staying in but I ran away.

It became exhausting. I was taking drugs that kept me awake and I was being passed around between men. Soon I started to become delirious – I had been awake for days, I wasn't eating properly. I was still too young to know how to look after myself. After what seemed like a week, we left the hotel. I didn't know where we were going. Chrissy appeared to have it all covered. We spent the following days with men and with older friends she knew.

One afternoon we were in a part of London called Camden Lock, near a canal, when Chrissy ran into a gang she owed money to. There were four of them, two boys and two girls. In their late teens, they were aggressive and demanded the money. For the first time since I'd met her I looked at Chrissy and realised she was scared. Suddenly she no longer seemed like a streetwise adult; she was a scared child. She tried to reason with them and explain she had nothing on her, but they grabbed her and started going through her pockets. Although terrified, I tried to stick up for her.

They started slapping her but she didn't fight back. They took the few notes she had left and then they threw her in the canal. Then they grabbed me, went through my pockets and threw me in too. The water was black, oily and freezing; we were only wearing skimpy clothes.

We both struggled to the side and managed to crawl out. Shivering violently and crying hysterically, I just wanted the warmth of home. I wanted to be in my bed with my dog.

'I'm calling the police,' I told Chrissy through chattering teeth.

'No, you're not,' she insisted. 'I'm not getting involved with the law. How much trouble do you think we'll be in? Do you want to go back into care? The next place they send you will be worse than Meadowside – you'll go to a detention centre.'

We argued and Chrissy stormed off, leaving me alone, bedraggled and scared. I was terrified the gang would come back and also scared that I had caught something from the filthy water.

The whole incident had been witnessed by many people. It happened in daylight in a very busy part of town. I had no idea where to go and, as I started to walk off down the road, huddled over to try to retain some body heat, a woman who had been watching from a bus stop across the road walked over to me. A big black lady, she was carrying several brown paper Primark shopping bags.

When she called me, I stopped. She looked me up and down, tutting.

'You're too young to be homeless,' she said sadly, shaking her head slowly.

She rummaged through the bags she was holding and thrust some clothes at me.

'Take these,' she said. 'God bless you.'

She handed me a pair of leggings, some socks and a sweater. I took them gratefully and thanked her.

But I had no money and nowhere to go. I felt trapped – I knew that if I went back to Oxford I would have to return to the gang, and I didn't want to go to a detention centre, like Chrissy said.

A few days before we were pushed in the canal, we had stayed with a man Chrissy knew. He owned a fried chicken shop nearby. A pervert, he was connected to the network we had been passed between but she seemed to know him better than the other men and at least he fed us. It was the only place I could think of that I knew nearby, so I went there.

He welcomed me in when I walked through the shop door and took me upstairs to the flat he lived in. It smelled of fried food but it was warm. I couldn't stop shaking – the cold had sunk into my bones and I felt like I would never be warm again. He gave me food and told me he would go out later and buy me some more clothes. Then he told me not to leave and said that he would look after me. He begged me to stay and told me the best way to get warm would be to drink – he had different bottles of booze and told me to help myself. He poured me a vodka and Coke and made sure the glass was half-full of vodka and half-full of Coke. I drank and he poured more.

In the four days I was with the man he got me drunk a lot. One night he took me out to Embankment to watch the fireworks on the banks of the River Thames. There was a big group of us – young girls and men. This man was an abuser, too, and he had a partner who came to the flat occasionally and didn't seem to mind me being there. The group were all strange – all drug addicts and drunks – and I felt increasingly unsafe and uncomfortable as the days wore on. The man was desperate for me to stay and I felt trapped because I had no money and nowhere else to go in the city.

Eventually Chrissy turned up at the flat. She didn't say where she had been but said it was time to go: the money had run out and she seemed anxious to leave London. I didn't want to stay with the man and so I did what I always did when my options had run out – I called Mum.

Her voiced cracked when she heard me on the phone.

'Where are you? Are you safe, are you in danger?' She told me later about the lengths she had gone to in order to find me. After the incident at the canal, she was contacted by the police. One of the witnesses had reported what had happened and the police had studied the CCTV footage and recognised me. They had told Mum and she had journeyed to Camden to try to find me. For hours she walked the streets, showing shopkeepers and passers-by photos of me to see if anyone recognised me or knew where I was. At one point we later worked out that she passed the chicken takeaway when I was in it – we were literally feet away. She became convinced that I was dead.

When she heard my voice the relief was overwhelming.

'Are you coming home, Lara? I'll come and get you,' she said.

But I had one condition.

'I'll only come if my friend can come back too,' I said. I wanted to make sure Chrissy was safe – I couldn't look after her, but I knew Mum would. She agreed and I told her we would meet her at Paddington station. She got the first train she could to London.

When she saw the state of me she fought back the tears. I looked washed out, dirty and tired; I hadn't bathed for days. I was wearing clothes that made me look like a prostitute.

'Where have you been? Why did you run away?' she asked as she hugged me tightly.

She would have known just by the sight of me what had been happening, but still I denied everything and told her I had been with friends.

'Who are these friends?' she demanded.

'They are just friends, Mum. People I know,' I told her. I could feel myself getting angry and she sensed this and tried to calm the situation.

'Have you eaten?' she asked.

She then noticed Chrissy.

'I'd better take you back as well,' she said.

When we got back to Oxford, Mum notified social services. Two ladies came round and started trying to explain that Mum needed to fill out certain forms and follow protocol if she wanted to foster Chrissy. Mum became exasperated as she tried to explain that she had removed a vulnerable child from an unsafe situation and was now looking for help and guidance from them, not for permission to foster her. They should have been thanking her.

Listening to them waffle on about regulations and hearing the way they were speaking to Mum, I got angry. I was eating a sandwich at the time and, in a flash, I picked up the plate and threw it at one of the ladies. Then I began yelling at her and threatening her and she ran out of the house, closely followed by her colleague. Eventually Mum had to meet them down the road with Chrissy, who was taken off and ended up in another placement.

A while later the police arrived to question me: they wanted to know where I had been, what I had done and whom I had met. They were trying to protect me and discover if crimes had been committed but I didn't trust them and so I only gave them vague details. I told them about the man I had stayed with and gave them the name of his takeaway outlet. I gave two statements and they also questioned Chrissy but, as far as I know, nothing ever happened as a result.

The care order still stood and so, a few days later, I was sent back to Devon to finish my placement. Within the system kids are shipped around while people in offices try to find somewhere for them. No one seemed to know what to do with me.

I was sad to be leaving Mum and she was worried sick, watching me leave because she feared I would run away again. She tried to argue that the problem was not our relationship. We had spent a lovely couple of days together: she took me to the cinema to watch one of the *Ice Age* films. I slipped back into the life I should have been leading – the life of a child.

But social services thought they knew better and so, once again, I was escorted across the country by security guards.

When I got back to Meadowside Chrissy was no longer there and I never ran away again because I didn't want to be on my own. Other kids came and went. After a few days, a teenage boy came in. I got distressed; I became aggressive and I refused to eat. It unsettled me being in close proximity to any male, no matter how old he was. When he left a week later, I settled down again. On my own, I got on with the staff and did the lessons I was supposed to do.

Mum came to visit me. On several occasions she drove all the way down from Oxford and at weekends I was allowed out to go and stay with her. She always worried about my appearance. I was wearing clothes that were way too small and tight for me; also I dyed my hair purple. She would remind the staff that I was still only 13 and demand to know why they allowed me to wear the sort of clothes I was wearing. They would tell her I was a young adult and it was my choice, so she bought more age-appropriate clothes for me.

So the days dragged on. The original eight-week agreement would have finished before Christmas but, as I went missing for over a week, I was allowed home for the festive season but had to return in January for another week. I left to return to Oxford and, while everyone else was trying to stick to the resolutions they had made, I fell back into the same pattern. Mohammed called, and I went. The gang had too much of a hold over me and two months in Devon had done nothing to break the spell. Mohammed knew when I was back. He lived so near that he would pass my house and, within days of my being home, he began texting. The helter-skelter started up as if it had never stopped.

'Be here at 4, you have work to do, you little whore,' the first message read. My heart pounded and I broke out in a sweat. Nothing had changed. Dutifully I went.

My master was calling.

Chapter thirteen

SKIN TRADE

The gang believed they were untouchable. I heard Mohammed once brag that the day he was caught by the police would be the day he died. That mindset made him dangerous – he believed he could be as violent and as blatant as he liked.

Mohammed knew I feared him and he trusted that I would never grass on him. He began to involve me in some of his business dealings; I was completely under his control.

One day he took me to one of his business meetings. It was in a house in a dodgy part of the city called Divinity Road; it was a meeting about drugs. Mohammed had fed me some before we went there to make sure my mind was fuzzy enough not to retain too much detail. The house belonged to a lady called Rachel – I had met her on several occasions when she came to the flat to buy drugs and later I worked out that she was a female groomer. She would help the gang recruit girls by identifying possible targets, gaining their confidence as a mother figure. Many years ago, she would have been me: a vulnerable child sucked into a dangerous world. An addict and a prostitute, she sat there in her bra and knickers, spaced out and waiting in anticipation for some free drugs.

Mohammed was meeting another man there. He walked in and looked like the caricature of a pimp: he wore a huge fur-lined coat and oozed seediness. By the way he was talking, it sounded like he was the drugs boss. The meeting was about how he and Mohammed could get people to courier their drugs without looking like what they called 'bait'. They wanted to get me to ship them around town – I suppose they trusted me because I was always with Mohammed or Spider and so submissive they knew I wouldn't tell anyone if I was caught. Already Mohammed made me take small packages from the flat to people waiting in cars outside so I was complicit.

The threat of violence wasn't the only thing I had to fear: Mohammed continued to remind me what I had become. He undermined me and told me everyone would know I was a prostitute and an addict and, even if I did tell anyone what was happening, I wouldn't be believed anyway, because of what he had turned me into. At one stage, I did try to stay away; I had a moment of clarity and realised how dangerous and out of control my life was becoming. For a few days I tried to ignore his calls, which had become increasingly threatening. Then one of my friends called. I knew Briony from secondary school and she had been surfing the internet and noticed something about me online.

'Have you seen what's been posted online?' she asked.

She gave me the address of a page on YouTube and told me I needed to look at it.

I typed the details on my laptop and watched in horror as the crudely made video loaded up: it included photos of me. It said I was a crack addict and a prostitute; it gave my address. Shocked and scared, I was certain where it had come from and why it was there: it was the gang's way of bringing me back into line. They were yanking the invisible lead, which kept me connected to them.

A reporter at the local newspaper, the *Oxford Mail*, was tipped off about the content and came to see Mum. He said they would not run the story but warned it was also on Facebook and Myspace. The police also got involved and had it taken down; there was no investigation. The day I found out about it I went straight round to Mohammed, apologised and told him I wouldn't leave again – I knew it was a warning and a demonstration of how much control they had over me.

There was a constant, implicit implication that they owned me and that I owed them. They held me in a jail they had built in my head. Whenever I was made to meet men, they would tell me that these people had travelled long distances to see me at expense. They had paid for petrol or accommodation. I knew they were making money from me – I would see it being handed over. It made me feel dirty, like a piece of meat. Once, when he was drunk, Mohammed told me I was worth £250 a time or £500 for the whole night.

For Mohammed and Spider, it wasn't about sex, prostitution or trafficking, it was about making money from me. Every now and then Mohammed would have sex with me. It was another way for him to exert his control over me. I found him repulsive but I had no choice, and he knew: I was just a commodity. The men who turned up knew this too. They were not introduced to me, my name was never mentioned; they just came in, sat down next to me and started touching me. They did it right in front of Mohammed. I recoiled but he fed me more drugs and so I let the men get on with it. High and drunk, I closed my eyes and I couldn't feel anything.

Sometimes, after they went, he would rub his hands.

'Nice little bonus,' he'd say. He was talking about the money. I'd walk past the river on the way home and wonder if I'd die if I jumped in.

The guys were all races and ages. Most didn't undress. I hated them touching my face and my hair because that was what Pat used to do at Terri's when I was little. I flinched – it was a business transaction. Afterwards I felt disgusted: I wanted to bathe, I wanted to be clean. Then I wanted to die.

After many months, I didn't feel anything anymore: I was a husk, dead on the inside. I wasn't making rational decisions about my life and I didn't care what happened to me. One day, after I had been with men for the gang, I went home and started to cut myself in my bedroom. I broke a glass and cut into my arms and wrists with the jagged edge – I did it because I wanted to feel something but I felt no pain at all. I hoped someone would notice and ask me what was wrong. Mum saw the cuts and she cried, and then she hugged me and then she told me off.

The more I became involved, the more I was expected to work. Several months after I had first been sold and a few weeks after returning from Devon, I was trafficked outside Oxford for the first time. Mohammed sent me. Early one evening he texted me and told me to meet him at the flat. He didn't explain what was going to happen until I got there and had smoked crack.

'Get on a train at Oxford at 7.45 and go to Paddington station in London. Make sure you are waiting outside the McDonald's there at 9.30,' he told me. 'Don't do anything stupid. I'll know exactly what you are doing and, if you misbehave, you're in a lot of trouble.'

He didn't come with me and he didn't give me money for the fare: I was expected to dodge the fare and, if I got caught, it was my fault. Instead, he sent me with drugs.

Mohammed sent the man who was meeting me a photograph of me via text so he would know who to look out for.

I did as I was told and found myself standing nervously in the busy station, waiting for the stranger who was going to take me and abuse me. Tiny and 13, I felt exposed but the concourse was so busy, no one registered me – I was just another face in the crowd. I was shaking due to the combined effects of the cold, the nerves and the drugs, which were now wearing off.

A man in his forties, wearing a suit and an overcoat, sidled up to me. Slightly overweight, he wore glasses and was clean shaven.

'Can I take your coat?' he asked.

He didn't introduce himself or say my name at that point. Later I learned that this was because, if I was being watched by the police and it was obvious he knew who I was, it could be used as evidence that he was buying me.

I pulled my coat up around my neck; it was freezing.

'No thanks, I'll keep it on,' I said.

He gestured for me to follow him and we walked out of the station to a parking bay, where he had a car waiting. I got into the warmth.

He tried to make conversation but I wasn't talkative. He talked about the weather and the traffic; he didn't tell me who he was and I didn't offer anything about myself – we both knew why we were there. He took me to a very posh flat in a place called Elephant and Castle; it was very different to what I had been used to. He was perfectly polite and offered me food and a drink. I turned down the food but I had a drink to steady my nerves – I knew that I would be staying with him for the rest of the night because there was no way of getting back to Oxford until the following morning, and that's what I did. The man had clothes for me to wear; I wore them and he abused me. The following morning he drove me back to the station.

On the way back to Oxford I told myself that it hadn't been so bad – there was no violence, the man had been polite. Compared to what I'd come from, the guy who met me at the end of the platform seemed like a nice man. That was how warped my perception had become. In reality, every man who touched me was a disgusting paedophile, but in my head some were much nicer than others.

When I got back, I went straight to Mohammed and he sent me off to Cowley Road, where Spider met me and took me to another man. I must have been making them thousands of pounds – it cost them nothing except drugs and alcohol. It cost me my sanity, my innocence and my childhood.

The trafficking became as regular as the selling. I was sent backwards and forwards to London. It always followed the same pattern: I got the same train and waited outside McDonald's at the end of the platform. I would be taken away by one man, and sometimes I would have to meet someone else after he had finished with me so he would either drop me off, or someone else would come and pick me up. I was kept topped up with drugs as I was passed between perverts. They usually had certain clothes and underwear they wanted me to wear, which was usually suggestive.

Sometimes they seemed remorseful. They knew what they were doing was wrong and they seemed sad about it. Some apologised and tried to ask me whether I was okay. Other men seemed lonely; they were not always after sex. Some just wanted to take me back to hotel rooms and talk to me. Mainly they were older men. Some were creepy, others desperate. One man told me he had recently been widowed and he wanted me to wear one of his dead wife's tops. I shuddered at the thought and, while I felt sorry for him, this time I refused. He wasn't violent, he was just a sad old man. I begged him not to tell Mohammed and he agreed.

Usually the ones who wanted me to change into a costume – such as school uniform – were the ones who didn't want anything of a sexual nature from me. Some would even say sorry while they abused me.

On one occasion there was a younger man. I don't know how he was involved but he took me to his mother's house and told me not to go back to Oxford: he knew what a dangerous situation I was in.

'You need to get away,' he told me. He explained that I could stay in London with him, and that he would get me a flat. His concern seemed genuine but still he was an abuser who wanted me to be with him. At no point did he offer to take me home or to a police station. All the men would have known I was underage, even though none of them asked. Even with the clothes and make-up on I looked my age.

In London the men were not Asian, they were Mediterranean, black or Arab. Before each journey to the city, Mohammed would get me high and he would give me drugs to take while I was there. I was sent off with Class A drugs, like other children get sent on outings with packed lunches. One time he got me so high before I was trafficked I was found unconscious on the street near the station by a young man who took me to hospital. I don't remember the journey or what happened when I got to the station. I woke in a hospital bed with Mum sitting next to me. I was questioned by police but told them nothing: my only concern was that I knew I was going to get a beating because I had messed up.

What made it worse was that, because I was so ill, Mum decided to take me to my uncle's house in Somerset to recuperate. We were there a week and all I could think about was what was going to happen to me when I went back to Oxford – I was actually anxious to get back, just to get the beating out of the way.

The day I got home, he was there, the omnipresent voice on the end of my phone.

'Get your arse round here!' he snarled.

When I got to the flat, he seemed to have calmed down.

'Have a seat,' he ushered.

I sat down gingerly on the stained sofa. The chemical sting of crack smoke hung in the air.

'I'm sorry, you gave me too much...' I started.

He was behind me so I didn't see the vodka bottle as he brought it down on the back of my head. There was a sickening thud and I was propelled onto the floor by the force of the blow to the back of my head.

'Don't ever, ever do that again, you little whore!' he screamed. His face was contorted in an angry snarl and flecks of spit flew from his mouth. 'I will slit your throat.'

I curled up into a ball and sobbed. My head was pounding. He had used the blunt end of the bottle and it hadn't smashed so there was no blood. I held my head in my hands to try to protect myself and felt a hard lump where the bottle had made contact.

'I won't do it again,' I promised through shuddering sobs.

Both Mohammed and Spider wouldn't think twice about hitting and slapping me. They did it to keep me in line. Sometimes the beatings were sustained. Other times, when I was lucky, they would slap me once and that would be it.

I had no one to turn to and Mohammed's violence left me feeling shaken and isolated. Part of me still wanted to believe that he was my friend and that I could trust him.

Away from the gang, my other life was equally messed up. As the trafficking escalated, I had what would be my last contact with Terri. It was arranged to be held in a shopping centre in Birmingham. She was high when we met and heavily pregnant – she looked worse and worse every time I saw her. At that point the relationship between her and Mum was strained because during one of her infrequent phone calls she'd started ranting at Mum, and Mum had put the phone down on her. Since then she had been frosty.

Kirsten was at the visit too and we went bowling. We ran off and didn't go back until Terri had gone – we used to run off a lot together when we had contact visits. On one occasion, we had an overnight visit and had been booked into a hotel in a service station. We ran off so much that a social worker had to keep guard, with Mum outside the room we were in.

I found it very difficult to be with Mum and Terri at the same time. I wished I could just leave that part of my life behind: Terri belonged to Lauren, I was Lara and I had a mum. It must have been really hard for Mum – she knew what had happened to me because of Terri and to a large extent she was having to deal with the consequences of the damage done to me in those early years. Yet still she sat in those contacts being polite. She was doing it for me because she believed I should maintain contact. She told me that it was important to keep in contact with my birth family and has always encouraged me to keep them in my life, right from that first night when I moved in with her and we lit the candles on the cake to signify the important people in my life. That made me feel anger towards Terri because she would never have found it in herself to be that selfless.

Terri gave birth to a boy a few weeks after the contact. He was born with a range of life-limiting disabilities, which was presumably because of her lifestyle. He was immediately taken into care and now lives with a wonderful family who love him and take care of him.

Terri called soon after he was taken away; she wanted a favour from me.

'Go and see your dad – he's got some money I need you to pick up and post to me,' she said.

It was counterfeit money. During the call, I tried to confide in her again about drugs and what I'd been doing.

'Crack is really good,' she repeated. 'What are you worried about, you Fat Jabba?'

That was her nickname for me: 'Fat Jabba'. She'd started calling me it when I'd put on puppy fat at the age of six; she enjoyed putting me down. Years later, Kirsten showed me a letter Terri had written to her explaining that I had been a mistake and I was never wanted.

During the phone call I lost patience with her.

'I wish you'd just leave me alone and die!' I told her before hanging up. It was the last thing I ever said to her. After that I didn't have contact with her and a year later, when I was 15, I found out she had died. I was by myself in the house, Mum was working. The phone rang: it was my sister (she was living in a care home at the time). She was hysterical.

'Mum's dead,' she sobbed down the phone. But I only had one mum, the one who had said goodbye to me that morning when she left for work. That was whom I initially thought she meant and my stomach turned.

'What...?'

'Mum's dead,' she repeated.

Then the penny dropped – she meant Terri. Still, I didn't believe her. She made a habit of saying dramatic things for attention.

'I don't believe you.'

Then she screamed down the phone at me and I heard the handset shift. A woman came on the line.

'Hello, Lauren.' I hated being called Lauren. 'I work at the home where Kirsten lives. I'm so sorry to have to tell you this but it is true: your mother died last night. Is there someone there with you?'

I was on my own.

'Someone will contact your adoptive parent and let her know the funeral details,' the woman explained.

Slowly I replaced the handset. I'd never been told someone had died before and so I didn't know how I was supposed to react. I felt upset and I felt angry; there was regret and relief. Then I started to cry and the sobs seemed to multiply in my throat like bacteria dividing until they were spewing out of me. I felt the urge to run away and bolted out the door into the street.

'My mum is dead!' I screamed over and over. I hadn't called Terri 'Mum' for many years and people must have assumed I meant Elizabeth.

Panicking and trembling, I ran to a neighbour – Hayley, who was lovely. She calmed me down enough to find out from me what had happened. Then she hugged me and told me everything would be OK and rang Mum. I was still in a state of shock when she arrived.

The details of how Terri died remained sketchy. She was in a rehab centre and had been found dead in her room; there were drugs there. I assume she overdosed.

Her funeral was held in a grey town in the Northwest; it was awful. I went with Mum and our au pair at the time, a lady called Sally. Mum employed her to help out around the house. Kirsten, Jayden, Nan and Granddad were also there. Harry and Jamie were not there. They were not told about her death until later; their adoptive family felt they were settled in their new lives and did not want to disrupt them. By this time, I had got over my initial emotional outburst: Terri wasn't my mum, she was just a person who had died. I was more concerned about being away from the gang and I couldn't wait to get back home in case my absence earned me another beating. Most of the other guests were a collection of alcoholics and addicts. Some people were drinking bottles of vodka behind the gravestones in the cemetery next to the chapel where the service was being held; they all wandered into the service at different times. Most of them looked half-dead themselves. Someone told me I looked just like her – I was on drugs myself at the time so I suppose I probably did. I got the impression that most of the people there were attending because it gave them somewhere warm to go and something to do. Apart from the screaming baby someone had brought along there was no real outpouring of emotion. Sad and surreal, it was what Terri had become: she was among her own.

The vicar said a few words – it was a load of crap.

'She was a devoted mother who tried her best.'

As the curtains closed around the casket and Terri's earthly remains were wheeled away to the fiery chamber inside the crematorium, his words rang hollow.

Chapter fourteen
SAM THE RAPIST

Each man I was forced to go with was a rapist but I didn't see it that way; I had a distorted value system. In fact I was sold so often that I placed no value on what was being sold, believing I was worthless. Abuse was a part of life, I managed to convince myself of that. I was more scared of the violence that would happen if I didn't comply than of the men who bought me.

The true implications of the life I was leading became horrifically apparent to me one day in 2006 after I'd spent a night on Cowley Road. I had gone there after being summoned by Spider. I'd been drinking; I was high. Out of my face, I was on my own. It was some time in the morning and I was walking around aimlessly, trying to clear my head before I faced Mum and lied about where I'd been. Someone behind me called out my name. I looked round and a man approached me. I couldn't place his face or remember whether I'd seen him before. I thought he was good-looking.

'How's Mo?' he asked.

'He's OK,' I answered.

'No, he's not, he's a dick,' he laughed.

I agreed with him, and laughed too.

He introduced himself as Bassam and asked if I wanted to go for a drink with him some time.

'Why not?' I said. He seemed like a nice man and we exchanged numbers.

But he didn't pester me. He sent texts every now and then asking how I was and what I was up to, and a couple of weeks after we first met, we agreed to meet up. I didn't think he was involved in the gang, even though he knew Mohammed.

Better-looking than Mohammed, he looked younger and fresh, clean-shaven. He did not look as though he was on drugs – he was well groomed, nicely dressed and he smelled clean.

He arranged to take me for a drink and by then I knew this didn't mean going to a bar or a pub. Unsurprisingly, we met in a house in Wood Farm. There were two other men there. I knew one – his name was Ali – but I didn't know the other one. They were obviously part of the drug side of the gang and I assumed Bassam was somehow linked in. While there, I drank a couple of cans of Stella and Ali and Bassam snorted cocaine. I didn't take any.

In the early evening Bassam suggested we go to a nearby guesthouse called the Nanford for more drinks. I agreed. I'd been there before – I'd been sent there to meet men. A flea pit, it had been highlighted in the national newspapers as being the worst hotel in Britain. It was described as a hellhole and rightly deserved the accolade. Rooms were around £20 a night. Spread out over four different properties, the rooms were dark, dingy and dirty. It looked as though the last time it was decorated was in the 1970s. There was a creepy man who worked there and didn't ask questions the times I had been taken there by men.

From the outside, it didn't look too bad but inside was grotty, rundown and the smell of damp pervaded everything; it was seedy. It was notorious in the town and the owners had been prosecuted years before for providing false addresses for benefit claimants and illegal immigrants. For years the local people had tried to get it closed.

This was where I ended up with Bassam. We travelled there from Wood Farm in a black cab that arrived to pick us up. On the way Bassam chatted to the driver in another language. I didn't know what language it was and didn't understand what they were saying. When we pulled up outside he told me to wait while he went in and got a key. A few minutes later, he came back out and ushered me round to one of the buildings at the side.

He took me to room number eight and he had drink and drugs with him. We both had a drink and Bassam had more cocaine. I didn't have any. The room was big, but grim. There were three beds in it, all covered with matching brown sheets. The carpet was spotted with stains and there were patches of damp on the walls.

I knew why we were there and, after more drinks, in the early hours I had sex willingly with Bassam. After that I'd had enough and that's when things changed.

Bassam carried on drinking and taking drugs and was becoming crazy – weird, forceful and aggressive. He kept telling he wanted sex again; he started pushing himself on me and he was stocky and powerful. I was scared and I told him to stop. He began grabbing at my breasts and throat.

'I don't want to,' I pleaded with him. 'If you do it, you will be raping me.'

But that made him mad and he punched me hard in the face. I screamed and started flailing at him in an effort to get him off me. It only made him more aggressive. He smashed me repeatedly in the face and the head. Screaming for him to stop, I lied and said that I was pregnant. He knew I wasn't, stood up, grabbed my hair and pulled me across the room.

As I struggled on the floor, he raped me while he continued to hit me. He was in a rage, screaming at me. All I could do was cower and pray the onslaught would stop. At one stage he was so forceful I cried out and he said he was going to make sure I never had children. I kept telling him he was a rapist and he clenched his teeth down on my breast. I tried to get out, but he dragged me back and beat me harder. He told me he was going to kill me.

Just when I thought it was all over he raped me again and continued to beat, punch and kick me. I tried to scramble away and he grabbed my leg and started beating me with a glass ashtray. Then he head-butted me; he was possessed. After that he dragged me into the bathroom and threw me down into the shower cubicle. I smashed my head on the porcelain and as I lay there, dazed and sobbing, he urinated on me. The onslaught went on for several hours and I was terrified I would die in that room – I couldn't get him off me.

He must have run out of energy because eventually the physical attacks stopped and he became verbally abusive.

'You're a whore and I'm going to kill you!' he shouted. I stayed still and tried to stop myself from crying in case the sound of my sobs antagonised him.

I realised I must have been there for hours because a faint morning light was beginning to filter through the curtains. Then I heard a commotion outside: voices and the crackle of a radio.

'Police! Open the door,' someone called. For the first time since the ordeal started Bassam looked worried.

'It's the police, they are here for you,' I told him. The relief I felt was immense. I started to call out but Bassam grabbed me by the throat and put his other hand over my mouth to muffle my voice. I heard the sound of a door being forced and waited for them to come in and save me. But they didn't: they raided the room next door. I heard them look around and then I heard them leave. The sound of their radios echoed down the hall.

Bassam held me down until he was sure they had gone and released me. I didn't care if he caught me, my instincts took over and I jumped up, grabbed a towel from the bed and bolted for the door. I didn't look round to see if he was following me and ran down the stairs and into the car park.

'I've been raped, he's going to kill me!' I screamed.

It was light outside and people were starting to make their way to work. They walked past, looking at me strangely. No one stopped to help. Barefoot, bloodied, I was in obvious distress. I heard Bassam call out from behind me.

'Come back!' He was laughing.

I glanced over my shoulder and he was hanging out the window of the room.

I wanted to find the police – I knew they couldn't be far away because they had only been there minutes before so I ran into the main reception.

'Help me, please, he is going to kill me! I've been raped,' I begged hysterically.

The man told me to be quiet but didn't seem to be taking me seriously and instructed me to wait in a store cupboard. He shoved me into the tiny space, which was full of catering-sized tins of marmalade.

Someone must have called the police because within minutes the door opened and a police officer beckoned me out. It was Becky, a WPC I knew from one of my missing episodes. I begged her to call Mum and she did. Grabbing the phone from her, I screamed and sobbed hysterically down it. I couldn't get the words out. Mum said later that she had never heard me so distressed; all I managed to get out was that I'd been raped and was in a hotel on Iffley Road. Mum said she was coming.

I must have looked awful. Tears and snot smeared my face and I was crying uncontrollably.

'He's going to kill me,' I kept repeating.

Becky held me gently by the shoulders and made me look at her.

'It's OK, we have got him. He has been arrested; he cannot hurt you,' she said.

Mum arrived a short while later. I collapsed in her arms when I saw her.

It later transpired that the police had turned up at the hotel after another guest called them because he had heard me being attacked. He was a businessman who was there for the night but he was not sure what room the noises were coming from and so the police turned up at the wrong door.

There was a 999 recording of the witness call, which I heard later. He had a West Country accent.

'I'm just calling to report what may be an emergency in Oxford,' he told the operator. 'I was staying in a place in Oxford – I've left now but I could hear a woman getting slapped around next door to my room. It was 20 minutes ago. I've left because I didn't want to hear it. It sounded like the guy had a prostitute in his room and started turning a bit sour on her.

'She was screaming. I could hear him slapping her. It sounded like there was a lot of messiness going on in there; she was shouting.'

Once I knew that Bassam had been arrested, I calmed down. I was still naked apart from the towel and I just wanted to go home and climb into bed. The adrenaline coursing through me had started to subside and I was beginning to ache. Every part of me hurt where he had attacked me and forced himself on me. But there was a process that needed to be followed: I had been the victim of a serious crime.

'Lara, love, this is very serious. He can't get away with this and the police need to be able to do their work and get evidence so this man can pay for what he has done to you,' Mum reasoned. 'It's important they examine you.'

I couldn't bear the thought of being touched again. Although exhausted, thirsty and hungry, I knew Mum was right and I trusted her and agreed to be medically examined.

This meant that I had to be taken to the force's rape suite, the custom-made facility I had gone to before. In effect, my body was a crime scene and so I couldn't do anything to contaminate it. It was the middle of November and frosty and all I had on was a towel – I wasn't allowed clothes because they needed to preserve the evidence. I was led out of the hotel and into the police car, where I had to sit on a plastic bag. It was early morning on a weekday and Oxford was starting to come to life. I was so traumatised I didn't even notice the early morning commuters beginning to make their journeys to work.

The rape suite was in a former council house on one of the main roads into Oxford and there was no parking outside so I had to walk to it wearing a towel, crunching barefoot through the frost in the rush hour. Sex crime victims who need to be medically examined must be seen by a registered forensic medical examiner (the police have to find one from a register the force holds). But the Oxford-based examiner was not available on the morning I was attacked and the nearest one they could find was based in Northampton. It was early morning and I waited for three hours before he arrived. I was starving and one of the officers swabbed my mouth for evidence, which then meant I could at least eat and drink, although I still could not wear clothes and had to sit on the same plastic bag to preserve any evidence. Leaning on Mum's shoulder, I drifted in and out of sleep.

Eventually a man in late middle age arrived. The fact that he was old made me nervous and his bedside manner didn't help: he was pompous and rude. The police were delighted to see him because they had waited so long. He introduced himself, then turned to Mum and said curtly: 'Mother, I presume.' I could see her bristle.

The examination was humiliating and uncomfortable. He conducted it in a businesslike manner. After a few minutes his mobile phone began to ring. I was shocked he hadn't put it on silence but what was more shocking was that he left me on the examination table and answered it. Then he started arranging a golf trip for a group of men with the caller.

When he hung up, he carried on the examination but his phone rang again. Once more he stopped what he was doing, left me lying in stirrups and walked over to the window to get a better signal. It was incredibly insensitive and afterwards Mum made her feelings plain.

By the end of the examination I'd had enough. Exhausted, aching and miserable, I wanted to go home. The police asked me if I wanted to give a statement there and then but I didn't want to stay and told them I would do so later. This was a mistake because it gave me time to think.

Mum was very understanding and she didn't push me. When we got home, I was still tearful.

'Can I sit on your lap?' I asked her.

'Of course you can, dear,' she told me.

Like a little girl, I climbed onto her lap and curled up, sucking my thumb while she stroked my hair and gently rocked me back and forth. She started singing nursery rhymes.

Whenever bad things happened that was where I found peace and calm: on Mum's lap being rocked like a baby as she sang lullabies to me. Her face would be etched with worry and she would stroke my hair and tell me everything would be OK. I don't know how she held it together. Pure love radiated from her.

Chapter fifteen
LARA VS LAUREN

The next morning I struggled to move. I was aching and the bruising had started to come out. There were angry marks, cuts and scratches on every part of my body. The police came and wanted to take statements and photographs of my injuries.

Already I had started to have doubts. Bassam was obviously connected to the gang in some way as he had mentioned people he knew whom they dealt with. I would have to go to court and give evidence. What if it came out in court that I took drugs? What if all the other stuff came out, details about the men? And the gang would know I was a grass. How would they react to that? And what if the case collapsed, like it had against the other man? There were too many ways it could all go wrong.

I convinced myself it was all my fault for going with him in the first place.

The police explained there was a lot of physical evidence and that Bassam was saying the sex was consensual. Mum could tell I was becoming doubtful about going ahead and tried to reassure me that I was doing the right thing but she didn't want to push me and she told me that ultimately it was my decision and she would support me, no matter what. I didn't appreciate it at the time but the support Mum showed in such testing circumstances was amazing.

I gave a brief statement and the police said they would come back in a few days.

A few days later, I was out in town and ran into a girl I knew. Her name was Vicky and she was one of the kids I hung around with. She was a tearaway, a binge drinker and a troublemaker.

'I heard about you and Bassam,' she said. 'I've just started seeing him.'

My stomach turned. How could she get involved with such a vile man?

'He phoned me yesterday and he was in tears,' she said. 'He's in a real state. He wanted me to speak to you – the thing is, it all got a bit out of hand. Did you know he has two young children?'

I didn't.

'Those kids are going to grow up without a father if he gets sent to jail,' she continued.

I knew how that felt – I'd grown up without a dad too.

The conversation was left hanging but the seeds of doubt had been sown in my mind. I couldn't be responsible for leaving two children to grow up without a father.

So I made a decision: I would drop the charges and withdraw the statement.

When the police came back to question me further I explained that I didn't want to go through with it. They asked why and questioned whether I'd been threatened. I clammed up and told them nothing and so, without the co-operation of the victim, they put the case on file.

The officer in charge was disappointed. 'We have enough evidence,' he said, 'certainly to get him on a charge of sex with a minor. The evidence will always be there so, if you change your mind at any point, we will take the case up again.'

A few days later, I found myself drawn back into the gang and their activities. It started as always with a text. I obeyed and made my way to meet Mohammed and the selling began as if nothing had ever happened. To me the only way out was death. I was brainwashed – I knew they had big families and networks and I was scared.

The point was brought home to me a week or so after the rape when I was in the flat, drinking with Mohammed, and Bassam walked in. I immediately recoiled and he started laughing. Mohammed joined in.

'Alright, bro?' Mohammed said.

'What…?' I was confused.

'We're brothers, you dumb bitch!' laughed Bassam.

It made me angry. On some level, Bassam getting away with it made me feel even more helpless. There was nothing I could do to get away from the situation and in a fit of anger I stormed over to Bassam and slapped him across the face.

'You raped me, you bastard!' I said.

He stopped laughing then and raised a fist to hit me. I cowered and Mohammed stood in the way. He stared defiantly at his brother and shook his head. At the time, I thought he was protecting me out of feelings but he wasn't: I was his property and he didn't want me damaged.

Bassam backed off and then started taunting me.

'How did you enjoy your shower?' he sneered.

Mohammed laughed at the reference. Bassam had obviously told him all the details of what had happened in the Nanford.

After the rape, Bassam seemed to become more involved with the gang. I found it intimidating and have no doubt it was another subtle way of controlling me and reminding me that I belonged to them.

At home Mum was desperately trying to stop me disappearing. I would go almost daily and each, time I did, I would return in a state of anxiety. After each runaway incident I came back broken. Psychologically traumatised, I regressed to being a little child, sitting on Mum's lap and sucking my thumb. Sleep became a real problem. I used to sleep in my mum's bed with her – I would start off in my own room and try to sleep but would be tormented by anxiety and panic. Then I would go up to her room, creep in and ask, 'Can I sleep in your bed?' She would open her arms and say, 'Of course you can.' I started to take my own duvet with me so I wouldn't steal the covers from her. Sometimes we'd sit up and have hot chocolate and biscuits, and she would talk to me. She tried to get me to tell her what was happening. Sometimes I nearly did as I was dropping off. At night I started to think and I hated being on my own. When I slept, I dreamt of faceless men.

But Mum couldn't have done anything to stop me – I was hell bent on destruction, my actions were nothing to do with her. I had to go out otherwise they would have come to my house to get me. Even now Mum is convinced she could have done more but she couldn't have; she couldn't restrain me because I hurt her. When she locked all the doors and windows, I broke out. I chiselled the window locks off and I broke the door, desperate to get out, even though what waited for me was abuse. There was nothing anyone could have done to stop me.

To this day, I have a lot of guilt about the way I treated Mum. There was always an expense and I never thought about it. I broke things and smashed them up but the emotional expense dwarfs the financial one.

I did things to Mum that were horrendous – I said nasty things to her, I told her I wished I was back in care, I told her she was a useless mum. All the while I could see my words hurting her. When I argued, I became physically violent. I used to bend her fingers back until they cracked if she tried to stop me leaving; I tried to push her down the stairs. I broke her belongings – I once threw a vase against the wall in the middle of a row, I smashed a laptop up, I stole from her. The anger was fuelled by the drugs. Often the police would be called; sometimes by Mum if I hurt her, other times by Jean or another neighbour. One argument started over cigarettes:

Mum tried to limit the amount I smoked and I exploded. I lashed out at her, threw an ornament and smashed a door. She told me she was going to call the police.

'Go on then!' I screamed at her.

When they arrived I resisted arrest and needed to be restrained.

Other times when I knew the police were coming I would sit in the bathroom and wait to be arrested.

I never meant any of it – I had no control over my emotions and I hated myself for the way I acted. If I hurt anyone else, I couldn't have cared less but, as soon as I hurt Mum, I was devastated.

I found it very hard to come down from violent episodes. Usually it ended up with me being arrested and I would only calm down after I'd been in a police cell for several hours. Jean would come to the station with me and be my appropriate adult (a legal guardian) because I was still classed as a minor in the eyes of the law and the offences were against Mum, and she was therefore classed as the victim.

I was never charged with anything but I was issued with a behaviour order, which was like an ASBO. It laid out what rules and behaviour were expected of me and I had to sign it. But I ignored it – I got away with a lot of things because the authorities suspected something else was going on. At one point Mum was third on the list of people most at risk from domestic violence in Oxford because of me.

The police in the town knew me by name. Even if I wasn't missing, I would be stopped in the street and asked whether

I had run away because I was so often reported as a 'misper' (missing person). Sometimes I was actually missing and they took me straight home. At one stage, Mum was reporting me missing almost every single day.

I got to know the lady who headed up Oxford's small Missing Persons Unit very well. WPC Jane Crump was a regular visitor at our house. She would attend the child case conferences about me, which were meetings between social services, the education department and the police to try to work out a plan of action for me. Jane ended up playing a significant role in my life and always suspected there was something much bigger and more sinister going on in the town, but she was a lone voice at the time.

She was short and lovely. She had a natural bubbly personality, which you couldn't help but warm to and she was understanding. Whenever I had disappeared and returned, she would come to the house and sit with me to chat. She would ask what was happening and try to gain my trust. I nearly told her once: it was a summer's day and we were sitting in the garden; I forgot I was talking to a police officer. We started talking about people I knew and I almost gave her a name. Somehow I stopped myself but she was very persistent.

Paul Phillips was another regular police officer in my life. I first met him when I was 12 and had gone missing; he took me back home. He was very easy to talk to and I could have a laugh with him and trust him – he was like a friend. Paul was very good to Mum and would often drop by to check she was OK. He had white hair and soft features and, even though he arrested me on occasion, he would never shout at me. I would see him in the street and he would stop what he was doing and come over to talk to me. He too knew something was going on.

'You got any news for me today?' he would ask. 'Gonna dob anyone in it for me?'

'No, Paul,' I'd tell him.

Once he found me in a crack den he raided. It was a flat belonging to an old man who was an addict – the gang had their claws in him and used his place to deal from. He was a sad man and lived there with his dog. I was friends with a young black drug dealer called Alan at the time. Like me he'd had a difficult childhood and was being used as a courier by the gang. I happened to be with him in the flat when the police raided. Alan had gone outside to make a deal with a customer and, as I looked absent-mindedly out the window, I saw about 10 officers in riot gear running up the short path to the front door. It was open but they still used a red metal ram to smash it off its hinges.

'Police!' they shouted as they filed in. I sat on the arm of the sofa and smiled at them when they came bundling in the lounge. They spread out quickly and started looking for contraband. Alan had been caught outside. One of the officers came over to arrest me. I recognised him as Paul Phillips and started laughing.

'What are you wearing all that for?' I said, gesturing towards his plastic shield and helmet.

'Try and take this seriously,' he sighed and then tried to get me to open my mouth so he could check whether I was hiding drugs in it.

The dog, an old Staffordshire Bull Terrier, was going mad in all the commotion. I was laughing, watching them as they hunted around for drugs. Eventually they found some small packets of powder behind photo frames and under a mattress in the bedroom. They also discovered a Samurai sword down the back of the sofa.

I was taken down the station, questioned and put in a cell. The police were always very polite to me and looked after me whenever I was pulled in. They offered me some food and drink. Later, when I was being questioned, I saw Alan and we waved at each other. He had told them everything and admitted his role: he went to jail but I heard he went gladly because it got him away from the gang and, while there, he studied law.

When I wasn't with Mohammed or being put to work couriering his drugs, life with Mum became normal – or as normal as it could be. My existence had become compartmentalised. I didn't like not having anything to do because I became bored easily and started thinking about the gang so I used to go out to work with Mum a lot to get out of the house and to get away from the pull of going to the drug dens. Whenever I was alone I felt vulnerable. Mum understood this and was good at distracting me. We used to have really lovely times – we'd go shopping or out for meals and to the cinema.

I was two people, living two different lives.

One life was lived as Lauren and I didn't like her: she was evil, horrible, violent and addicted to drink and drugs.

Foul-mouthed, she wore shed-loads of make-up and skimpy clothes; her hair was scraped back. She was not a nice person – she had no redeeming qualities. The other life was as Lara: she wanted a chance, she wanted to be happy and loved. If Lara and Lauren were two separate girls rather than sides of my personality, they would not have got on, which meant I was in a constant state of inner conflict. It was very confusing because I didn't know who I was. I kept getting drawn to being Lauren because I felt I had no choice: she was a product of my unstable childhood and never had reason to trust anyone. She was always let down and that made her hostile.

Lara was my new life – she developed as I grew up. Around family and decent friends I was Lara. Happy-go-lucky, friendly and open-hearted, she was loving and loyal and liked to have fun. Lara was the scared little girl who sat on Mum's lap, sucking her thumb: she craved affection but then she disappeared for long periods of time. Lauren wanted to be needed too, but in a different way.

Lauren belonged to the gang, she was their possession and plaything. When I was Lauren, my life was unimaginably dangerous – I still wonder how I never ended up dead. They used to test out new batches of drugs on me; they would get in a consignment and tell me to try some. I didn't care if it killed me. Often I had suicidal thoughts – I wished I could fall asleep and not wake up.

In turn the gang cared nothing about what happened to me or the people I knew. After the rape, Mohammed had become even more brazen because he knew that, even if

Mum or I did go to the police, I wouldn't go through with a prosecution – I was too weak.

Mum knew there were bad men in my life. The jigsaw of who they were was beginning to piece together. She knew Bassam, or Sam the Rapist, as I referred to him. And she had spoken to Mohammed on the phone when he had called the house, which he did frequently. She had demanded to know who he was and what he was doing with me. She knew him as Mo; she also knew he was a drug dealer because sometimes he would stand on the corner of the road and deal drugs near our house. Several times she warned him off. In response, he threatened her.

'I know who you are and I know where you live and, if you call my daughter again, I will call the police,' she once told him.

'Your daughter is a crack whore and, if you call the police, I will kill you both,' was his reply. She hung up. She never showed if she was frightened or angry.

Mum did report him but nothing happened because I didn't co-operate and this only encouraged the gang to draw me in deeper.

Chapter sixteen

HUMAN TRAFFIC

Mohammed kept me busy. He had a seemingly never-ending stream of customers to satisfy. Men would travel in from all over the country, from as far away as Bradford, London and Leeds. I was advertised through a network of people who all knew each other; ordered up like a takeaway via text messages. There were photos and obscene videos of me taken when I had passed out or been semi-conscious. These acted as a sick menu and were pinged out to punters before prices were agreed.

The guys who abused me had no personalities. I told myself they were robots because the truth was too hideous to imagine. In reality, they were probably men with wives and children who held down regular jobs.

Mohammed's business interests were national. The range of the trafficking eventually went beyond Oxford and London and I was sent to other cities: Liverpool, Leicester, Bradford. One day I was told to be at the corner of my road. I left home and within a few minutes, a car pulled up. Mohammed was in the passenger seat. I knew the driver – a man who was often with Mohammed, and whom I assumed was something to do with the drug trade. There was another man in the back seat; he looked smart and older than the others. He seemed friendly. The car was shaking with bass from a rap CD that was blaring from the speakers.

'Get in!' shouted Mohammed.

I did as I was told and the car sped off.

'Where are we going?' I asked.

'We're going on a business trip,' said Mohammed. The others laughed.

We were in the car for over three hours. I sat in the back. Cocaine and cannabis joints were handed around. I didn't take any. The rap music got louder and, by the time we arrived at our destination, I felt nauseous – I still had no idea what we were doing but I understood that, if I was there, it would involve men.

I looked at the road signs. We travelled along the M40 to Birmingham and then up the M6 until we finally stopped somewhere in the Northwest.

We were in a residential street of good-sized houses. Mohammed told me to get out and the others followed. I followed him up the drive of the house we had parked outside. It was a sunny day and, as I walked towards the front door, I could hear music and voices. I could smell food; I realised I was hungry.

Mohammed knocked on the door and a middle-aged Asian man answered. They exchanged a few words in another language and we were all led inside. It sounded like there was a party in the back garden of the house.

Mohammed grabbed me and took me through to the back of the house, where a barbecue was in full swing. There were around 20 men there, ranging in age from early twenties to sixties. They were a mix of races but predominantly Asian, Arab and black. There were three other girls there, each one sitting quietly next to a man. They all looked like me: young. Obviously teenagers, they were dressed like me in short skirts, push-up bras, heels and tight tops. Each one had her hair scraped back and was plastered in make-up. I'd been told what to wear when I got the message from Mohammed. It dawned on me what was happening.

I was there to be sold, as were the other girls.

'Don't talk to them,' Mohammed warned. 'And don't wander off.'

He put me on a sofa and got me a drink, which I accepted gratefully. I could feel eyes fixed on me; many of the men were staring hungrily. I felt self-conscious. As I scanned the room, I saw one of the girls had a baby. She was holding it and I assumed it must have been hers; she couldn't have been older than 15. After a while I saw Mohammed deep in conversation with another man. They kept looking over at me. I'd been involved for long enough to know they were negotiating. After a few minutes, the man walked over to me.

'Come on,' he said, gesturing for me to follow. I looked over at Mohammed, who indicated that I should go. He took me into one of the bedrooms in the house, where I was abused.

It happened several times that day, with a different man each time.

Mohammed was in a good mood on the way back – it would have been a lucrative trip for him. We arrived in Oxford in the early hours; I'd been drinking all day to blank out what was happening. I was worse for wear and he ditched me by the side of the road, about a mile from my house.

After that, there were other barbecues in other parts of the country. I worked out that they were like shop windows, where girls were promoted because, after each one, trade seemed to get busier. I never knew I was going or for how long, and they were the only times I ever saw other girls.

Most of the time I was too out of my head to comprehend the scale of what I was involved in. It was organised and vast. There were hundreds of men and apart from the people in control, such as Mohammed and Spider, I never saw the same face twice.

Back in Oxford, I was also expected to work more for Spider and Jammy. Most days or nights, after I'd been to Mohammed, I was sent to Cowley Road where they operated. Usually by then I was a zombie, out of my face. Spider didn't care what state I was in; he put me to work whenever he had a punter. He had an evil stare that made me believe he was capable of anything. I couldn't say no – he was terrifying.

One afternoon I was in a kebab shop on Cowley Road and so drunk I fell asleep, slumped on the table. I've no idea how long I had been there when I was woken by someone yanking me violently by my hair off the chair. I yelped and instinctively lashed out at whoever it was. I was dragged up and out the door and I thought I was being kidnapped. As I was marched across the pavement to a waiting car, I screamed.

'Shut up, bitch!' I heard someone shout.

Suddenly, as the fog of boozy sleep cleared, I recognised the voice: it was Spider. He threw me in the back of the car, where there was a man. Then he got in the front and waited while the man raped me.

When he was finished they threw me out onto the road, where I sat in the gutter, crying. No one did anything. After a while, I walked home.

I was just an object; I was grabbed from wherever I was and taken to car parks or guesthouses. Spider and Jammy didn't sexually abuse me but they may as well have: they would pin me down and other men would rape me.

I had no idea what a normal relationship was meant to be like. All I had known was older, abusive men and so, one day, when a man whom I knew bought cannabis from Mohammed approached me on the street, I thought nothing of it.

I'd seen Chris Regis in passing on a few occasions. He looked like a thug; he was certainly much older than me. At the time, through the messed-up prism of my experiences with men, I thought he was attractive. A large, muscular black man, he dressed like a yob in baseball caps and trackies – the equivalent of mutton dressed as lamb. He worked as a security guard. One day when I was standing outside the Vodafone shop in the city centre we bumped into each other. We acknowledged each other and made small talk. He asked for my number and said perhaps we could hook up one day and so I gave it to him. To me he seemed like a decent man. I realise now how warped that was: I was 14, he was in his thirties. Although he didn't know exactly how old I was when he started chatting me up it was obvious I was very young.

When he called a few days later and asked to meet me I agreed. Chris invited me round to his flat and I met him there; he smoked cannabis and we had a drink together. He seemed genuinely interested in me and his flat was clean and comfortable. I spent a couple of hours with him, we talked, nothing else happened and he didn't press me. When I got up to leave, he asked if he could see me again. I agreed.

Later that evening I was at home in my room when the landline rang. Mum answered it and I could hear her becoming agitated.

'She is 14, are you aware of that?' she told the person on the other end of the line. 'You are not to see her again or contact her, or the police will be called.'

When she hung up, she called me.

'That was a man called Chris,' she said. 'Apparently you left your phone at his house earlier. He was calling to let you know.'

'He's just a friend, Mum,' I said defensively.

'I doubt that,' said Mum. 'How old is he?'

But I didn't know; I explained he was just a friend again.

'You might think he is a friend, Lara, but why do you think a man who is clearly older is interested in a 14-year-old girl, and what were you doing at his house? Don't you realise how dangerous it is, going to older men's houses?'

Mum didn't know the half of it.

She told me she had arranged to meet him and retrieve the phone, which she did later that night. Once again, she told Chris in no uncertain terms that he was not to contact me again. He explained that he had no idea how young I was.

Despite being told that I was a minor, he did contact me again and I began to see him on a regular basis. Perhaps I thought he could protect me. He was a big man who could look after himself and I was being sold and trafficked more and more. I was disappearing for days and returned from those trips covered in bruises and clearly drugged or drunk.

Nobody except Mum was doing anything. The police and social services knew something very serious was happening but claimed nothing could be done because I would not co-operate. It was a failing that let the gang carry on with what they were doing with impunity. The authorities figured that, without a complaint, there was no victim and hence no crime. They tried to get me to talk but I wouldn't, and so they raised their collective hands and did nothing. I have often wondered since why no one had the presence of mind to put me under surveillance. If they had done so, it would have been easy to see the horrific pattern unfolding. Instead, the authorities were getting desperate and the only thing they could think to do was to send me away again, but this time they sent me to a secure unit for my own safety.

I'd been away for several days and returned battered and exhausted; I'd been sold repeatedly. Mohammed stayed with me all the time to make sure I was drugged and obedient. I wasn't allowed to sleep and, even if I had, I was too scared: I was delirious with exhaustion and drugs. I remember snatches; I remember being in a room with several men. I watched them, they were chatting and laughing, and sometimes they tried to involve me. So I sat and waited for the inevitable.

When I got back, the decision had been made.

Mum explained to me what was going to happen: I would be taken away for eight weeks and given support and structure; there would be counselling. She was visibly upset when she was telling me this because it was an extreme step. But by then, I knew something had to change: if I carried on the way I was going, I would be dead within months. I looked horrendous, like a ghost. When I gazed in the mirror, I didn't recognise the wretched creature who stared back through dead eyes.

I sat down with Mum at the laptop and googled the term 'secure unit'.

'They can be to protect young people who are placing themselves and others at risk of harm through a range of behaviours. In these instances the unit is not used as punishment but to ensure the young person's safety,' I read.

The description went on to explain that secure units were designed to protect children and to help them address the issues that result in them being there.

The unit I'd been booked into was called St Catherine's Secure Centre in St Helens, Merseyside. I would be staying in a lodge for eight weeks, which specifically looked after girls and young women who had been subjected to exploitation and violence in the community.

I'd been placed under a secure accommodation order by the courts and, although the decision had been made for me, I wanted to go. When the time came to leave that evening I had packed my bag and was sitting outside on the pavement, smoking a cigarette and waiting to be taken away by security guards. Both Mum and I were tearful – I knew this wouldn't be an easy placement.

I slept most of the way and got to the centre when it was dark. From the outside, it looked like a modern school or clinic. Inside was like prison – it housed runaways and so security was of course tight. All the doors were locked, sleeping rooms were locked, and the toilet windows were locked. There was an on-site psychiatrist and rigid rules to follow.

One of the first things I had to do was undergo a physical examination in case I had any medical conditions that needed treating. This included taking a pregnancy test. I also had an initial psychological assessment, which involved a lot of questions and was carried out to deem whether I was a danger to myself and others.

'Do you have any suicidal thoughts?' the psychologist asked.

'I don't know, I've only just got here,' I answered.

The centre was divided into residential units in different parts of the modern building, which was roughly the size of a school: I was in Brontë Unit. There was another unit for mentally disturbed girls. Each unit had a living area with bedrooms, or cells as I thought of them, and a communal area with a television and kitchen and dining area. There were six bedrooms in Brontë Unit, laid out along a corridor; also an open unit that housed 24 children and young adults.

I was taken to the unit where I would be spending the next two months, led through steel doors that clanged shut into a comfortable dorm with six bedrooms in it and a main living and kitchen area. My bedroom was sparse. I had a thin mattress on a metal bed frame, there was a metal shower and toilet and a CCTV camera on the ceiling. There was no TV or hi-fi, like in my room at home – they were privileges and I was told I had to earn them (it took about four weeks of good behaviour to earn a telly). My bedroom window had bars on it. Although every effort had been made to make the space appear comfortable and homely, there was no escaping the fact that there was no escaping.

Bedtime was at seven and, in the evenings, we were allowed to watch television in the communal room and go out into the yard. I wasn't allowed to wear the clothes I'd arrived in, just in case me or any of the other girls used the cord in the hooded tops and trackie bottoms to hang ourselves, or 'ligature' as it was known. All I had brought with me were trackies and they all had string waists so Mum bought me some new clothes with elasticated waists when she came up the next day.

The rules were strict. There were levels of behaviour – one to four – and good behaviour accrued privileges. If I fought, I lost the privileges I'd gained, which included television time and exercise. Any infraction would result in my being downgraded a level. In the unit we weren't allowed pens or anything sharp we could harm ourselves with and we had plastic cutlery at meal times.

The days were filled with lessons, activities including arts and drama, exercise and counselling sessions designed to make you look at your life and think about how and why you behaved in the way you did. It was like a live-in school with teachers who came in.

The unit was full of crazy girls and I felt exposed and vulnerable – I'd been in adult company for such a long time that I was mistrustful of anyone my own age. Most of the girls were runaways like me.

Georgina was 15 and came from Manchester; she had HIV. She was so disturbed, she heard voices and saw things. She would post paranoid letters under my cell door telling me 'they' were going to kill us all but I didn't know who 'they' were. Georgina stank of urine and it transpired that she had lots of sexually transmitted diseases. She had gorgeous long black hair, which she would not wash. In the end, I was the only person she got close to and she let me wash her hair. She'd been placed in care when she was very young. We had our differences and her moods swung wildly, but when she was stable we got on well. In the end, she confessed that she was being trafficked but I could tell by her attitude and the way she looked as soon as I met her that she was like me; she was also doing crack. She latched on to me and no one else.

Soon after she arrived, we had a fight. She threatened my key worker, the woman assigned to look after my welfare. I got on well with her and was protective so I lost my temper and threw a chair at Georgina; I had to be restrained and lost my privileges. It took a couple of weeks to earn them back again.

Georgina wasn't really a danger to the other girls, she was more of a danger to herself. Sometimes she would be completely normal, other times she would babble incoherently. She used to talk about seeing rats at night, it scared the crap out of me. I was in the cell next to her and she would appear at the door. She was so white and, with her black hair, she looked like a ghost. I would tell her to be quiet.

One day I woke up and she was gone – she had been sectioned.

Holly came from a normal background and loved her mum and dad but got involved with the wrong people. She was white but spoke like a Jamaican and was very racist towards white people. We used to take the mickey out of her. Constantly trying to ligature, she was involved in a gang. Aged 15, she was very tall, about 6ft 2in. She wore her trackie bottoms rolled up on one side, like a gang member, but she was the least menacing person you could meet. That didn't stop her trying to be intimidating, though. I got in a fight with her, too – she was trying to throw her weight around and I told her to stop bullying people. When she started to argue back, I told her I couldn't understand a word she was saying so she tried to strangle me.

After fights I never bore a grudge. It was a status thing – if I got beaten up, I got beaten up. I'd shake hands and that was it.

Suzanne was 17 and beautiful. A little thug, underneath she was so kind-hearted – she had time for everyone. She lived with her mum and dad and partner in Norwich; she was only there for a couple of weeks.

Then there was also Kerry who came from Wales and had gone crazy when her mum had a baby. She had mental health issues.

We all became very close in the end.

I celebrated my 15th birthday in the unit and we had crisps and did limbo dancing. We also organised and performed a musical show. I sang 'Amazing Grace'. I liked the song; I remembered it from when I was made to go to Sunday School when I lived with Graham and Pauline. I wasn't a bad singer.

We had some fun times in the unit. One of the workers there was also an extra on *Hollyoaks* and a dead-ringer for Ricky Whittle, who played Calvin Valentine. He was gorgeous and girls would argue on purpose in the hope of being restrained by him. Along with most of the girls in there, I had a crush on him. He was very good at his job as he would always be able to calm the girls down if they needed restraining. I used to tell him how fit he was and he would get embarrassed. We watched him while he was eating his lunch and he would get really embarrassed and leave the room.

I had regular counselling sessions in which the counsellor tried to discover what was making me angry – I was so guarded that the probing made me angry! The female counsellor tried her best. She was non-judgemental and acted concerned. She asked a lot of questions and tried to get me to talk about Terri and Shane and my background, but I didn't divulge anything – I liked to be left alone by the adults. I was starting to form relationships with people my own age, which I hadn't done before, and the staff were really good and noticed this and encouraged me.

I can't say that the eight weeks were a pleasant experience but at the time they were what I needed. It was a life-changing experience, mainly because I was around kids my own age and in a strictly structured environment, where it was hard to stray. There I had to confront my demons because there was no running away. Away from drugs, I got healthier. I put on weight and had a routine: I got up, went to lessons, had lunch and went back to lessons. Good behaviour was rewarded, I learned. Eventually I reached the top level of privileges and was allowed out of the unit into town with a member of staff to have my cigarettes. That happened the week before I left and I was the only one in the unit who made it that far.

The secure unit gave me space for reflection and for Mum and me to rebuild our relationship. We hadn't really got to know each other – I'd only been with her for a year and a half before Mohammed groomed me. Mum would have known more of Lauren than Lara. In fact, the only time I was ever Lara was when I was with her. She saw what I could be, which is why, no matter what strain she was put under, she never gave up on me.

Mum came and picked me up. She brought the dogs in the car to meet me. It was lovely to see her, and lovely to be going home. There was an air of optimism on the journey: I could see a different outcome for me, I felt much better and more positive about my situation. I felt older and stronger. At that stage, if someone had asked what was happening to me, I would have spoken to them.

In the unit, perhaps for the first time in my life, I saw a brighter future with Mum. I was focused on the there and then and I hoped everyone had gone away and forgotten all about me by the time I got out. Deep down I knew they wouldn't have and there was a nagging fear in my gut: I was nervous about leaving because I knew what I was going back to.

With hindsight, I wish I'd stayed at the unit longer. If only I'd been there for a few more weeks, I probably wouldn't have become involved with the gang again.

Chapter seventeen
A HOPE

Things did change for a while when I got home. I got a place at a private tutorial college to try to catch up on my schooling, of which I had missed several years. More than any subject I enjoyed art; I was good at it and I enjoyed it, too. It was the only thing I ever stuck at and maintained an interest in. Mum loved art too – it was something we had in common and together we would visit galleries around Oxford. I was not at the college for long, though: away from the confines of the secure unit, I had trouble maintaining a routine. It was not the sort of place I enjoyed. It was structured and I didn't like being told what to do. I found the subjects boring and I had no respect for the teachers. I was supposed to be there to do my GCSEs but, after a few weeks, I began to skip lessons.

I also had an Outreach worker assigned to me. Her name was Alexa and it was her job to try to keep me interested in education and maintaining some kind of continuity in my studies. I saw her once a week and went to an education centre. Alexa used to take me out on educational trips. They were more like fun, however, and we went to places such as zoos and museums.

Mum was gently encouraging but could see me already sliding back into old habits. Although I'd been away, in Oxford nothing much had changed. It didn't take long for Mohammed to start to get in touch. The texting began and I tried to ignore it, but the messages became increasingly threatening. For outsiders it may be hard to understand why I kept falling back in with the gang. I was brainwashed and I was ruled by a mixture of fear and warped loyalty. I felt I belonged to them, and I knew that even if I changed my number they knew where I lived and would come and collect me.

'Do you want everyone to know what you are?'

'Don't ignore me, bitch.'

I started to panic – I knew he would turn up at the house and so I went to see him. At first, he didn't ask anything of me: he gave me drink and I accepted. The next time he gave me drugs and, within a few days, I was back under the fearful spell.

Finally the stress took its toll on Mum. She'd been battling against me and the system for so long, crying out for action and trying to be heard so it was inevitable that her health would suffer.

I was at home one day with a friend and Mum arrived home early from work. She was acting very strangely.

'I must go and make some muffins,' she said.

I looked at my friend and frowned – Mum didn't seem quite with it.

She fussed around but didn't appear to be achieving much and was confused by what she was doing.

Mum is a good cook and, when she came out of the kitchen an hour later with the worst-tasting muffins I have ever eaten, I knew something was wrong. I have no idea what she put in them. She started trying to explain what she had used but she kept forgetting and getting her words jumbled. It was such odd behaviour that there was undoubtedly something seriously wrong with her.

'Mum, are you OK?' I asked.

She looked frightened.

'I don't think so,' she answered.

And then I noticed that her face was starting to droop on one side.

That's when the wave of panic hit me. She was having a stroke and I knew enough about strokes to realise how serious they were. I must have seen something on TV about them once.

'Mum, what's wrong? I'm scared,' I cried. 'You can't have a stroke!'

I always knew I relied on Mum and for years I had taken her for granted and thrown all her love and care back in her face, time and time again. In those moments, the realisation that she would not always be there to pick up the pieces hit me like a sledgehammer in the chest.

'You can't leave me!' I sobbed.

Terrified, I ran to get help from Jean, our dependable neighbour, who came in and called an ambulance. There was little I could do to help and I was in such a state I would have caused more disruption, so it was decided I would stay at home while Jean would go with Mum who was taken to hospital. I didn't know whether she was going to live or die. She was gone for a couple of hours and the wait for news was excruciating. My friend stayed with me and tried to reassure me that it was probably nothing.

When Mum walked through the door later that evening, carrying fish and chips, I almost collapsed with relief. Jean was with her and explained that she had suffered something called a transient ischaemic attack, which is a mini stroke. It was only a minor one and, thankfully, she would recover fully. Mum had been driving when it happened and had returned home, disorientated.

I didn't know how to react to this close call and, instead of telling Mum how much I loved her and how worried I'd been, I got angry. That seemed to be my default emotion. Everything made me angry and, despite the anger management classes at the secure unit, I had trouble overcoming it. I felt angry that I relied on Mum and terrified that I could have lost her. That fear made me angry and the anger seemed to drive me back to Mohammed and Spider.

A few things did change, though. After the secure unit, the trafficking didn't start again. I believe it was because I was getting old; I was now 15. Instead, I was sold in Oxford by them. And increasingly, Mohammed began to sexually abuse me himself. Each time he made me feel dirty and worthless. I wanted an escape and I found it in Chris, who, despite being warned off and told my age, continued to contact me.

I saw more and more of him and our relationship developed into a rough approximation of boyfriend and girlfriend. He was 32 and I was 15. It took me many years to understand that my relationship with Chris was abusive and that he was a paedophile. At the time, I was so brainwashed and so used to being with men far older than me that I couldn't see anything wrong with the situation. I convinced myself that Chris cared for me and, in his way, he did. Perhaps he was just as warped as I was. In my eyes he was kind-hearted, fun and bubbly. And, most importantly, he wasn't violent and didn't force me to do things I didn't want to do.

He had four kids by two different women, he worked as a labourer as well as a security guard, and he lived by himself. Chris knew I knew Mohammed and he also knew Mohammed was bad news and dangerous but he wasn't scared of him. I don't know if he ever realised I was being exploited by Mohammed. I never told him but he did warn me not to see him and also told Mohammed how old I was. Partly he confronted Mohammed out of concern for my safety, and partly for selfish reasons: he was possessive and didn't want me seeing anyone else. His intervention on my behalf did nothing to scare the gang off, though – Mohammed simply gave me a slap for getting involved with another man.

Around this time, there was another older man in my life whom I cannot identify for legal reasons. I saw him on a few occasions while I was seeing Chris, whom I discovered later was also seeing other girls.

I would go to Chris after I'd been with Mohammed. He would cook me food and straighten me out, as I was usually drunk and high. It was my first proper relationship but I didn't have feelings for him: I wasn't attached, he was someone I could go to.

Chris never tried to hide me away, which is why I now wonder whether he had convinced himself that there was nothing wrong with seeing an underage girl. We went out on dates – we went to the cinema and the park, for meals and we had picnics. I always felt uncomfortable when we were out because I knew people would be looking at us. It was obvious he was much older than me and I was also worried that one of the gang would spot us. Not that Chris would be concerned – he showed me attention and he got me away from the drugs for a while.

I never thought of the future and took each day at a time but Chris was hopeful that things would develop between us: he thought we were going to be a forever couple. He told me he loved me, I laughed at him.

He bought me nice clothes as gifts and I felt that he was a decent guy; he had genuine feelings for me. The age gap didn't shock me, it didn't even register – I knew it wasn't normal but then again my life had never been normal.

A year after I had got out of the secure unit, that was my life. Periodically I was with Mohammed: when he beckoned, I went running. I was taking fewer drugs and I was in a relationship with an older man, sometimes seeing another. While I never allowed myself to feel positive, my life felt more stable than it had for a long while. I was taking more care of myself and had started to look less like a drug addict. And then something happened that changed everything. It was Christmas 2007; it had been a lovely festive season. Mum and I spent time with family in Somerset. She always made sure Christmases were magical. When I first went to her, I was never able to understand or enjoy the wonder of the festive season – I didn't like surprises, I had no sense of wonder. If there were presents in the house, I would find them and then argue with Mum about having them there and then.

'But you've bought it, why can't I have it now?' I would complain. Eventually she left Christmas and birthday presents at her work.

The Christmas in question was perfect. However, after New Year I had started to feel sick, mainly in the mornings. For the first few days, I convinced myself I had picked up a bug, but the nausea persisted and I began to worry.

I had convinced myself over the years that I could never become pregnant. Too much damage had been done. Although I wanted to have a family in time, I thought that was another part of my life the gang had stolen from me.

I continued to feel out of sorts and eventually I told Mum, who advised that perhaps I should take a pregnancy test. She remained calm and supportive but I can imagine inside she was thinking, 'Whatever next?' I never denied that I was having sex with someone, even though I was underage.

Mum bought the test and was with me when I did it. We were in the house in Oxford. It was a crisp January day and my heart was pounding as she and I stood in the kitchen and focused on the little white plastic stick I held in my hand. The blue line appeared very quickly. I thought I was going to pass out and then I burst into tears. At first I wouldn't believe it, and then I wanted to do another one just to be sure.

'We'll wait another couple of days and I'll do another,' I said. Instead, I waited a couple of hours and did one and again it came back positive. The following day I went to the doctor and he confirmed that I was eight weeks pregnant.

I didn't know what to think: it was a huge shock. There were so many questions going round in my mind. Mercifully, when I was abused, the men always wore protection. It appeared to be an unwritten rule. There were two men who could have been the father: Chris and the other man I had seen occasionally. I believed it was Chris, and I knew Mum would want to know. I could hardly keep it a secret – but did I want a child?

My life was a mess, *I* was a mess – how would I ever be able to bring up a baby? But all the time there was another thought formulating in the back of my mind: a baby could be an escape.

Mum was non-judgemental and supportive.

'I will support you whatever you decide,' she said. 'It won't be easy but I will be here for you.'

It took me a long time to actually realise it was happening but when the shock subsided over the following days I knew increasingly that a termination was not an option. I wanted a baby and the more I considered having one, the more excited I got. I thought it would change everything.

'That's it, now you can get on with your life,' I told myself.

It was a way out.

I told Chris I was pregnant a week after it was confirmed; I called him and asked to meet him. I was honest and told him I thought he was probably the father but there was a chance he wasn't. Then he told me he would be there for me. He planned to stick around but he knew in his heart of hearts that we wouldn't be playing happy families, and so did I – he had left all his other children. But for the time being he was happy in his cosy delusion and told me he would support me. He began to get obsessive about what I was eating and drinking; protective, like he was my dad rather than my boyfriend. I became less and less interested in him. As the pregnancy progressed, I became hormonal and, frankly, I was horrible to him.

I got big quickly. I was so skinny it was painful and now I had a huge bump. I suffered with morning sickness but it seemed to go on all day. But that did not seem to matter. I hoped that the baby would allow me to get on with my life. It was my way out. I stayed away from the gang. I stopped drinking but I was still smoking.

I loved going out and Mum helped buy stuff for the new arrival. The family were told and supported us both. It was decided that I would move out of my room and into the loft room, which was bigger. Mum and I decorated it in *Winnie the Pooh* wallpaper and stickers when I was four months pregnant. We went to Toy R Us and bought teddies. We also bought a cot, a Moses basket and tiny clothes.

Mum came to the scans with me and together we sobbed when we saw my baby's tiny heartbeat on the screen. I was 14 weeks when I had the first scan and my baby was perfectly formed. Mum burst into tears.

'Oh my God, it's a baby!' I shouted. At that point it finally hit me that it was real, there was a little person growing inside me. I was given copies of the scan and was so proud I carried them around with me. At the second scan I found out I was having a boy, which I had sensed from day one. I lay on the bed and the sonographer ran the sensor over my protruding belly. I could see him clearly on the screen, but at first he wouldn't uncross his legs.

'Have a drink of water,' she advised. I drank a pint and poked my bump and on the screen I could see him move. He was clearly a boy.

'He's certainly not shy!' laughed the woman.

In between the scans there were doctor's appointments, where I could hear his heartbeat. It was reassuring for Mum and me – she was always so worried about what was going on so when we heard his little heartbeat it was comforting. Each beat was filled with the hope that life would change for the better.

It was a lovely time for both of us. Mum had never had children of her own and in a way I think she lived that magical time through me. We bonded deeply and had agreed before the scan that, if it was a boy, she could choose a name and, if it was a girl, I would name her.

I hardly ever saw Mohammed during my pregnancy. He knew early on and he wasn't interested: I was of no commercial value to him when pregnant and also I did not want drugs.

I didn't crave them and being pregnant gave me the strength to stay away. He did get in contact regularly, however – he wanted to keep an eye on me to make sure I wasn't talking to anyone and to keep a hold over me.

He called and texted and told me to meet him. I made excuses. Usually I told him that I had a hospital appointment. I wasn't sold when I was pregnant; without the drugs and alcohol I was less easy to control and I think that made Mohammed nervous.

When I was seven months pregnant he texted and ordered me to meet him. I did as he asked.

'How are you?' he asked slyly. We were in Riverside Court and I had refused his offer of a drink.

'You look fucking massive,' he laughed. 'You know it's my baby.'

I wasn't sure if he seriously believed I was pregnant with his baby or not and scoffed.

'You have to have sex to make a baby.'

Mohammed reached into a pocket and produced a cigarette. Although I had given up drinking and drugs, I was having trouble stopping smoking and I took it from him – I was nervous being in his company, the cigarette would help calm my anxiety. He lit it and I took a drag. Immediately I realised something wasn't right. The smell of burned plastic hit my nostrils. I coughed out the smoke before it could sit on my lungs.

'You're sick!'

Disgusted, I flicked the cigarette at him: he had spiked it with crack.

He thought it was hilarious and doubled over, laughing.

Chapter eighteen
NOAH

Lauren Long was finally killed off in February 2008 when I legally became Lara McDonnell. It had been a long, hard road and part of her would remain, causing problems and upsetting what should have been a time for fresh starts.

That was the only way I could understand why I was drawn to the gang life. I was two people – I didn't understand that I had been the object of a methodical process of coercion and compulsion. Lauren was the part of me who was drawn to the gang, like a moth to the flame. She couldn't resist the lure, and she wasn't strong enough to break free; she was ruled by fear. In changing my name I had driven a symbolic stake through her heart.

When I finally became Lara legally, it felt like a relief: I was shedding a part of my life I didn't want anymore. For many years I had been ashamed of who I was. I didn't want to be associated with Terri and Shane, I didn't want to be referred to by the name they gave me – I didn't want to be anything to do with Lauren. I liked Lara, it suited me. There was never any pressure from Mum for me to change, she was happy with whatever I wanted.

The change, before I gave birth, also meant that my son would carry the name of my new family, something I was pleased about. Just to mitigate any problems, I had given Mum a list of names she could choose from and she chose Noah. Throughout the pregnancy he was known as 'Spuddy', however.

In a way I saw my son as my salvation: I hoped his arrival would solve everything. Already my pregnancy had had an effect on the gang. They left me alone through most of it and it also had a beneficial impact on my relationship with Mum – we had definitely become closer because of it. We had the best time in years: we were discovering each other, and it was new to us both. Together we went to antenatal classes and sat down and wrote a birth plan – I wanted an iPod with a calming playlist on it and a warm footbath in the room. Mum was wonderful. As a teenage mum-to-be I should have been worried, but Mum had told me she would support me and help me raise the baby. She expected me to stand on my own two feet – to carry on college and get an education after he was born, to get a job and support myself – but she would help me achieve this and I wanted to be a good mother.

Social services, who were still involved with me, were not so confident of my ability to be a good mother, though. They seemed to surface each time there was a drama in my life and midway through my pregnancy they took an interest in me again and held a case conference about me to decide what the best course of action would be. I explained that I was trying my best to stay out of trouble and look after myself, but they didn't have any faith in me. It was obvious they were concerned for my son's safety and I was scared they would take him away as soon as he was born.

'Why don't you just give me a chance?' I begged. But they were insistent that I shouldn't be the main carer and that the role should instead fall to Mum. They explained in no uncertain terms that, if I didn't agree to this, they would have to seriously consider their position. I couldn't bear the thought of my baby being placed in the care system like I had been and so, ultimately, I had no choice but to agree.

For obvious reasons I had no faith in the system and was angry about the intrusion. In my experience case conferences were exercises in buck-passing and finger-pointing. Social services would call for me to be sectioned and pass the buck to the National Health Service. Mental health would say I needed counselling, the police would say that social services were trying to shift the problem somewhere else and everyone would blame each other and miss the true nature of the problem: that as a vulnerable child from a neglectful background I had been targeted, groomed and exploited by a criminal gang.

I didn't like to be told what to do and I didn't respect authority, especially when it was so obviously lacking. During that case conference, I was handed a file that listed in black and white the details of my childhood. A long list of miserable experiences, it was the first time I had ever been presented with my own sad biography. I had never thought of myself as particularly unlucky or tragic but reading about incident after incident it did strike me what a difficult time I'd had and I was determined not to give my own child such an awful start in life.

I struggled through the spring and early summer of that year, getting bigger and bigger. It was becoming increasingly difficult to walk and I started to question how I would get to my due date, which was the end of August. When it arrived, the reason became apparent: at a check-up it was discovered my dates had been miscalculated and I was two weeks overdue!

I was scanned at John Radcliffe Hospital in Oxford to find out what the consequences of this oversight would be and it was discovered Noah was starving in my womb. The amniotic fluid that should have been surrounding and protecting him had gone and his umbilical cord was wrapped around his neck. It was decided that I needed to be induced the following night. I was terrified: clearly he was not very well.

I was taken to the labour ward, where the procedure to bring on labour was performed. It wasn't long before I started to feel the first contractions and the pain of them took me by surprise. Each one gripped me and sent spasms through my body. My head started spinning and I vomited. Mum was with me and looked on helplessly.

'What can I do?' she asked desperately.

But there was nothing she could do. As the hours passed, the pain grew greater – I had never felt pain like it. I was given gas and air and that made me violently sick as well.

We settled into an unsteady rhythm through the night. At each contraction I would wretch as there was nothing left to bring up and in between Mum would mop my forehead and try to get me to sleep. The birth plan went out the window – calming mood music was the least of my worries. It was a long labour and Mum slept on the floor when I managed to sleep. She was amazing – she wouldn't leave my side and knowing she was there made it bearable. Mum fussed and made sure everyone was doing their jobs properly – I felt I could get through it, knowing she was in my corner.

Noah was born on 29 August 2008 and he made a dramatic entrance into the world. I tried to get through it without pain relief but was suffering so much that I had an epidural. But I was weak and exhausted at the end and, as the cord was wrapped around Noah's neck several times, he was becoming distressed. At that stage the best course of action would have been a C-section but he was too far gone in his journey to the outside world. Throughout the final stages of the birth the delivery team tried to keep track of his heartbeat using a monitor in his head – it was like a metal needle. I was terrified and agitated and this was stressing him out. Mum was hugging me and telling me everything was going to be OK. Finally, I had to be cut while he was delivered by Ventouse forceps, which they had trouble attaching. I was losing blood fast and on the verge of passing out when he finally came out. I couldn't hear him cry and so I panicked.

'What's the matter with him?' I cried.

After what seemed like hours, but was probably only a minute he made a sickly little yelp. He was a poor little thing – his head looked like it had been scratched with barbed wire, where he had been poked and prodded. Towards the end of my pregnancy it had been estimated that I would have an 8lb baby: he was 5lb 14oz. Mum saw him first; I was close to collapse (I had lost two pints of blood and needed to be stitched up urgently). She held my baby while I was being seen to and eventually he was handed over to me, wrapped in a blanket and peaceful. He looked like the most beautiful thing I had ever seen. All too soon he was taken from me and whisked off to the special care unit because he had been through such a trauma.

He had to stay there for the first night and I was sent back to the maternity ward on my own. All around me mothers cradled their newborns. Mum wasn't allowed to stay so I was alone. The midwife took a photo of Noah, printed it out and left it by my bedside.

I was determined to breastfeed him and the nurses told me, if I managed to make my way to the special care ward, I could. As I struggled along the corridor, I was in a great deal of pain.

Noah was lying in a glass cot, nestled in a soft blue blanket. He was asleep. I looked at him for a long time and wondered what kind of a life he would have. The ward was busy and I wanted everyone to go away so there was just me and him.

'Hello, Noah,' I whispered. 'I'm going to be your mummy.'

The word held so much power. What kind of a mummy would I be? He had pulled the feeding tube out of his nose, a nurse replaced it and I gingerly picked him up and held him. I was scared to cuddle him in case I hurt him, he looked so delicate.

I stayed with him for a long time but felt myself drifting off and so I made my way back to my bed for a fitful night's sleep. Mum came early the next day and, because we'd had such a difficult day previously, the hospital allowed us to have a family room so she could stay the following night. I refused to leave until Noah was released and, anyway, I was in no fit state to be going anywhere. Later that day I was allowed to take him to the room and he slept between Mum and me: we were a little family unit starting life together. Mum and I were going to be his mummy and daddy together. Neither of us had any experience of children so after he was born we had a maternity nurse who came to live in the house. Mum paid her and she was there for four weeks to show us the ropes and taught us how to deal with the night feeds, how to feed and bath him. She arrived two days after he was born. Initially I breastfed.

We were both very protective of him, sometimes overly so: we used to make sure no one touched him with dirty hands or that, if anyone had smoked, they brushed their teeth before they went near him. When we got back from the hospital Mum wouldn't let anyone in the house for the first few days and whenever we went out in the car with him in the following weeks she only drove at around 20 miles per hour and slowed down further over speed bumps. Anyone who did come round to visit was carefully watched to make sure they held him correctly.

We settled into a routine and over the following months Noah got bigger and stronger. On the surface everything seemed as normal as it could be given the fact that I was a teenage mum but underneath it all I was struggling with my demons. I was still frightened of the gang and, after a couple of months, my fears became a reality.

While pregnant, I had been left alone. Mohammed contacted me every so often, just to check up on me and remind me of my place but very soon after I had Noah the pressure was back on. He called me at home to say congratulations and then in the next breath said, 'See you in about half an hour.'

As soon as I heard his voice my attitude and behaviour changed; I could feel the fear and anger take over. I felt helpless to resist, which in turn made me hostile towards Mum when she asked where I was going. I felt hostility to Noah, too – my little saviour had changed nothing.

When I went to leave I argued with Mum. She reminded me that I had a responsibility to my child and that I couldn't just walk off when I fancied it, which made me feel even more trapped.

'This is all your fault,' I hissed at him as I stormed out.

I realised I had been stupid to expect anything to change. I was never going to be allowed to leave: I knew far too much, I was trapped.

Mohammed was vile – he knew that I knew I couldn't escape. I was his property, and always would be. He tried to give me drugs then but I refused; he didn't push it further because he knew eventually I would crack.

The domestic bliss was shattered and over the following months I became depressed as the calls and texts from Mohammed became as frequent as they always had been.

Several months after the birth the men started again, too. If it was possible I felt even more worthless than I had before. Not only was I owned and used by the gang, I was also a failure at motherhood.

Postnatal depression set in. On some days I didn't want to get out of bed or interact with my baby; I was scared to bond, and I was scared to feed. Emotionally and practically, I pulled away from the situation. I didn't bother with feeding, changing, playing or cuddling him because I felt like I couldn't, and I wouldn't be able to do those tasks properly. I would cry for no reason.

Summoned by the gang more and more, I disappeared regularly. Under immense strain, I didn't know where to turn. I wasn't emotionally strong enough to cope and Mum ended up doing the majority of the caring; I resented her for this. I began to feel that Noah was more like a little brother than a son but I tried my best and there were times when I loved being a mum and could almost forget about the other part of my life. Then there would always be a call or a text that shattered the illusion. It pains me to this day but there were times when I resented Noah and I shouted at him. Whenever I did, he would look at me accusingly and then laugh.

Mohammed talked about him in the same way he used to talk about my puppy and Mum – in an underhand, threatening way.

'Wouldn't it be terrible if anything happened to your baby?' he sneered. I knew what the implication was; he didn't need to spell it out.

I didn't want to bond with Noah because I was scared he would get hurt – I found it very difficult, having someone who needed me so much and trusted me to look after him.

I had another problem, too. Chris had seen Noah once but was under police investigation for having sex with a minor. Mum had reported him when she realised I was seeing him before I fell pregnant, and for several months the allegation sat on file. But he was then arrested for another offence and the police decided to charge him with the sexual offence as well. I was called in to give a statement but Chris took it all in good grace and told me to be honest and to tell the truth about everything.

Although I was not seeing Mohammed as much as I had before Noah was born, whenever I did, it was a big session or something serious happened. I tried to stay off drugs but found it very hard and eventually succumbed to the constant pressure.

I had often been the gang's drug-testing guinea pig and, when Noah was a few months old, they summoned me with the promise of drink and a new batch of crack. When I walked into the Riverside Court flat, Mohammed was sitting on the sofa in front of the coffee table, on which sat a bag filled with off-white granules.

'We need to test this,' he sniffed. I was weak-willed and I did – I hadn't smoked crack for a while and, as soon as I inhaled, I felt my chest burn and my lungs tighten. But then, almost instantly, I felt light-headed and euphoric. The worries and stresses melted away.

'What's it like?' asked Mohammed.

I nodded and smiled, my eyes were rolling.

'Strong,' I said. The effort of speaking made me splutter but I didn't care.

He offered me more. I took it. Again, my lungs tightened. It became harder and harder to breathe – I felt like I was having an asthma attack and tried to regulate my breathing. Each time I inhaled my lungs burned but the drugs seemed to momentarily relax the tightness and so I continued to smoke them.

Mohammed could see me struggling for breath and did nothing except offer me more. I was wheezing loudly and he laughed.

I was in the crack den for what must have been a couple of hours and, as the drugs started to wear off, I realised I was in trouble. Struggling for breath, I knew I had to get away and so I staggered to my feet.

'Where are you going?' giggled Mohammed. He thought it was funny.

I lurched out the door – I needed to get home and to get help.

When the cold air outside hit my lungs I felt they were being gripped by a vice and then I really started to panic. I staggered the short distance home and fell through the door. Mum heard me collapse and rushed to help.

Between gasps, I managed to tell her I had smoked crack. I genuinely believed I was dying. My heart was hammering inside my chest; I thought it would explode.

'Goodbye, Mum,' I managed to wheeze.

She stroked my hair.

'You're not going anywhere.'

She called an ambulance and, within minutes, it was there. The paramedics put an oxygen mask over my mouth and nose, and I was helped into the back of the vehicle. Mum and Noah came with me – there was no one to look after him. I looked over at him and his little smiley face gazed back at me quizzically.

In hospital I was immediately put on a nebuliser and hooked up to a drip, which had an immediate effect. Already I could feel my chest start to relax. It hurt when I inhaled and I was kept in overnight. Jean came and got Noah, and Mum stayed with me.

When I was feeling better and had eaten she tried to broach the delicate subject of what had happened.

'Who did this to you, Lara?' she pleaded. 'Can't you understand how much danger you are in?'

But I couldn't. I always had a distorted perception of danger – when I was younger and was taken on contact visits with Kirsten we would both run off and often ended up chatting to older men. On one occasion we had been lured into the cab of a lorry after striking up a conversation with the driver. He could have taken us anywhere, he could have murdered us, but at the time it never occurred to me that I was in danger: it was an adventure. Mum would tear her hair out with worry. After that episode she showed me a news report about a girl who had gone off with a man and was raped and killed. Weeks later her decomposed body was found in the woods.

'Don't you understand, Lara? This is what could happen to you.'

But I didn't understand and I didn't actually care. Later in life I heard a theory that may have explained my behaviour. In the early years, when I was living with Terri and Shane, I was exposed to danger and fear on a daily basis. Most days my body was flooded with adrenaline to the point where I became used to it. Adrenaline acts in the same way as some drugs and people become addicted to it. Perhaps in those first years of my life, when my brain was growing, I became addicted to adrenaline and hence to danger.

Lying in a hospital bed after the crack overdose I started to open up.

'I think I'm getting addicted to drugs,' I told Mum, adding that Mohammed had given them to me.

'It was my choice to take it,' I went on.

Mum was in an awful situation: she couldn't stand by and let me continue to associate with people who were supplying drugs to me but she knew that, if she went to the authorities without my agreement and willingness to provide information, nothing would be done and I would turn against her. She would be sending me back into the hands of the gang.

'They are dangerous people, Lara – they don't care about you.'

She was right but I didn't realise just how much danger I was in or how to get out of the spiral I was caught in. At the age of 16 I was becoming too old for all their punters – they wanted young girls so instead Mohammed had started to use me for his own gratification. I never gave a thought to what would happen when he got bored with me.

While I was trying to pull away from the gang I was called to give evidence against Chris at his trial. I was required to give video evidence. The hearing was in Oxford and Chris was given a jail term after I explained that we had been in a relationship since I was 14. I explained that he was never violent or abusive and I was sad to see him go to prison; I knew I wouldn't see him again and I also knew that he would not be involved in Noah's life. There was still doubt that he was the father anyway. I made the decision to tell Noah the whole truth when he was old enough to understand and to let him decide at the right age whether he wanted to try to find out who his father was. At that point, I still couldn't accept that what Chris had done was wrong and, no matter how much Mum tried to explain to me that he was an abuser, I couldn't see him as one.

I turned 17 and was seeing the gang less and less. Financially I was becoming worthless to them: I was too old for their paedophile customers and I was also becoming older and stronger. I wanted it all to be over and they could sense it – I was coming up with excuses all the time. Ironically, the maternal instinct that had deserted me early on was kicking in and I didn't want to be away from my baby.

The coercion that had worked when I was younger was no longer effective. Instead, it was being replaced by threats. They tried their best to keep me compliant with drugs and at times it worked. Mohammed even spoke to me about recruiting young girls for him. The idea sickened me but showed he was always on the hunt for fresh blood. I was strong enough to say no. There was definitely a change in the mechanics of control. I had a deep sense of unease – I knew they were capable of extreme violence and I feared not just for myself, but for Mum and Noah, too. The best course of action would be to try to keep them at arm's length; to do as they told me when they were annoyed with me and hope eventually they left me alone.

But they didn't and when Mohammed called one day after a gap of a few months I felt it was best to go and meet him. My memories of that day are sketchy but I remember being taken in a car with him to a house in a place called Brasenose Driftway. Mohammed never drove, he got people he knew to drive him around and in this instance the driver was an old man he used as a courier. At some point during the day I blacked out. Snatches of memory have returned to me since. I remember coming to at one point in a room: naked except for my bra, which was around my ribs. Lying down, I turned and saw Mohammed behind me, penetrating me, grimacing through his black, crack-addict teeth. When he realised I was conscious, he pretended to lie down and be asleep. I remember vomiting.

Then I remember being at home, lying on the sofa. I remember Mum's worried face. I remember paramedics, I remember an injection that jolted me awake and then I remember hospital, where someone told me: 'You've overdosed on heroin. You are lucky to be alive – your heart stopped.'

I was horrified – I had died and been revived. I'd never taken heroin and vowed never to try it because of what it did to Terri; I thought it was a disgusting substance. Mohammed had spiked me with it. I don't know how much I was given but clearly it was enough to kill me. In hospital, one of the medics noticed I was bleeding and I felt pain below my waist. The horrific realisation dawned on me that Mohammed had given me heroin until I collapsed and then raped me. I wasn't surprised by the depths of his depravity and I started to resign myself to the fact that the only way I would be free of him would be if I killed myself.

Mum had told the police and they came to interview me. I didn't tell them who I was with at the time and there were so many gaps in my memory I could see by the looks on their faces that they knew it would be hard to make a case stick. However, a quick-thinking medic had collected evidence and they did have two DNA samples. Subsequent investigations discovered one belonged to Mohammed; it was never discovered who the other one belonged to. It was obvious that something had happened but by then I was 17 so they couldn't make a charge of sex with a minor stick. Eventually they decided there was no case.

But that incident changed everything. Over the years Mum had mentioned on several occasions that, if I wanted to move away, she would happily sell the house and we could make a fresh start. I had never considered the option before:

she was working and her life was built around Oxford. I didn't want her to uproot and go but I'd had enough and my life was in danger.

In hospital Mum mentioned it again.

'You only have to say the word,' she said.

I looked at her. She'd aged in the years she had known me and I'd done that to her. She had stuck by me and never let me down and all I had done was cause her heartache.

Overcome with guilt, I started to cry.

'I want to move,' I whispered through my tears.

For weeks afterwards I couldn't go out. I'd been raped repeatedly throughout my teens but this was different: I was traumatised by the thought that I'd been given heroin and by the evil of what had happened so I ignored Mohammed's texts and calls, which became increasingly aggressive and incessant. He would call the house up to five times a day; he threatened me and he threatened Mum. I think for the first time he was worried about what I might do and this worry made him mad.

'Answer me, you fucking bitch!' he'd scream to my answerphone.

'Get your arse to the flat, whore!' he'd order.

I was terrified. After the rape, I knew he would stop at nothing. I could easily have died and it would not have done the gang any harm if I had: it would have solved a problem. I'd just be another junkie who overdosed in a dingy crack den – a tragic, wasted life. The more I considered it, the more I thought it was a real possibility that they had purposely tried to kill me. They had threatened to do so on many occasions over the years. The older I got, the more my life took me away from them, and the more distance between us, the more dangerous I was to them.

The final straw came when Mohammed threatened Noah.

'You are going to die but, before you do, I am going to cut your baby's head off and send it to you in a suitcase,' he said.

White and shaking, I came off the phone. By then the house was on the market but I didn't know how long we would have to stay in Oxford. There was a 'for sale' sign outside that Mohammed would have seen and I was sure this had antagonised him even more.

I walked into the kitchen where Mum was feeding Noah. He looked so small and innocent.

'I want it to stop,' I told her.

And, for the first time, we went to the police together and I told them that I was being harassed and threatened. I gave them Mohammed's name and the address of the flat.

They acted quickly and took me seriously. I was half expecting them to ignore me but instead they hauled him in and told him that he was under no circumstances allowed to contact me ever again.

I like to imagine how quickly the cocky demeanour evaporated from his smug, ugly face when he realised that he could no longer control the girl he had used as his slave for four years.

Chapter nineteen
CHOOSE LIFE

We had several viewings and the house sold quickly. Mum had been there for over 15 years. She was surrounded by friends and I felt guilty that she was sacrificing all that because of what I saw as my mess. But she never breathed a word of regret and I think she was genuinely looking forward to a clean break.

In the seven years since she had adopted me her life had changed beyond all recognition. We had both been through more upheaval and drama than most people experience in a lifetime.

We set about deciding on where to move to. Both of us agreed it had to be far away and each weekend we selected a location and drove there to investigate. We travelled all round the country looking at towns and villages until we settled on a pretty market town somewhere in the Southwest. It felt friendly and safe and was far away from Oxford and the dangers that were there.

Mohammed knew we were moving and his threats continued until the day we moved. But the police caution seemed to work because now he never turned up at the house. He phoned regularly and I told him that the police officer who arrested him lived next door – he believed me.

The last weeks before the move were nerve-wracking. I tried to stay out of the way of people I knew as much as I could – I didn't want to be asked too many questions. I was very careful who I talked to. I had a small circle of 'good' friends and a wider circle of 'bad' ones; I only told a few of the good friends and my siblings whom I was still in contact with on a fairly regular basis.

Despite the nerves, I have fond memories of that time. Finally it felt like I was getting control of my life, something I'd never had. I was bonding with Noah too and became closer to Mum. We spent a lot of time packing up stuff and cleaning the house. I boxed up Noah's belongings and looked forward to making a new start. I realised that the strange feeling I had in my heart was optimism – I had only felt it before on the journey to Oxford when I first moved to be with Mum, and I liked it.

We were in such a hurry to move on that we didn't have time to buy anywhere to move into; we just wanted to get out of Oxford. Mum had friends in the town we were going to and they had kindly agreed to let us stay with them while we hunted for a new home. We had no idea how long this would take but we looked forward to house hunting together. I didn't care what kind of property Mum bought but asked that we move into a new one as I was afraid of ghosts.

In the days leading up to the move friends helped us pack. A few had stuck by me through thick and thin and they knew some of what I had gone through. I knew I could trust my closest friends and they promised not to tell anyone where I was going. They knew I was moving because of Mohammed but they didn't know the full story.

As a leaving celebration we had a big barbecue the night before we left and invited all the neighbours. We had drinks and music and said goodbye to the people who had been with us through the worst of the bad times; it was an emotional night. They had all been so understanding and had supported Mum through the trials of the previous years. It was a proper send-off and I had mixed feelings because my life in Oxford wasn't all bad. I had many very happy memories too and I couldn't help feeling bitterness towards Mohammed for the way he had hijacked my happiness and affected the lives of so many good people.

Having said my goodbyes, when the day came to leave I couldn't wait to get out. As we pulled away from the front of the house for the last time I didn't look back and, with each mile that passed, I felt a little lighter. If I had stayed, I would have died – I would have either killed myself or been killed by them. I think their plans would have been to keep me forever as their slave. I would have ended up like that other woman I met who worked for them or as a dead junkie, like Terri; I chose life instead.

We got to our destination and helped the removal men unpack the furniture and boxes that we would have to leave in storage until we found a new home. That night I went to bed exhausted but happy. The following morning I woke up and felt free and safe. For the first time in many years I knew I didn't have to worry; I wasn't looking over my shoulder. I had grown so used to being under someone's control the freedom felt weird. Noah was with me and we had our dogs and cat. We had a place to stay separate from the main house, which meant we had our own space and there was not so much pressure on us to move out quickly. I didn't ask Mum how she felt at the time but I think she was relieved. She had given up full-time work and was working on a freelance basis. She had to go back to finalise some of the details and I think she was just desperate to get it all finished.

We set about making ourselves anonymous. I got rid of my old phone and deleted all the 'bad' numbers from it so I wouldn't be tempted to contact anyone. I got a new number, which I only gave to people I could trust. There was no way Mohammed could contact me. I broke off my links and we went ex-directory. We took our names off the electoral roll and I closed my Facebook account; we did everything we could do to disappear. I made sure the location services were always turned off on my new phone so I couldn't be tracked.

Then I changed the way I looked. I took my piercings out and I stopped wearing make-up; I dyed my hair – I reinvented myself. We didn't tell the police when we left and by that point social services were off the scene as I was approaching my 18th birthday and no longer under the age of consent so they were not notified either.

If Mohammed did try looking for me, he would never have found me: I had vanished and I was liberated.

In the end, it took us six weeks to find a house and move in. It was June 2010 and we had the summer to look forward to. We were preoccupied with house hunting and getting to know the area. The people we were staying with had two large dogs and we had an indoor cat so at times it got hectic, but in a fun way. It was idyllic – Mum was happier than I had ever seen her; we both became a lot stronger. We spent quality time together and got to know each other again without the distractions we had faced in Oxford. When we found our house, we shopped for fittings and set up our new life. We talked about colour schemes and decor.

When we got the keys, our stuff was still in storage and it took a few days to arrange to get it moved, so on the first night we sat on pop-up chairs in the lounge with a picnic table.

I started thinking seriously about what I wanted to do with my life. I had left school and so I applied for a college course on public services but it was all theory and no practical training so I stopped going. I still found education hard; I was playing catch up because I'd been thrown out of school at 14 and had missed out on education full stop so most of the people on the course were younger than me. My ambition was to get a life, make decent friends, be a good mum and get closer to Noah and Mum.

I had a small party for my 18th and was taken to a champagne bar by Mum the night before. I didn't know anyone in the new town and at first I didn't want to make friends; I kept myself to myself. I found it hard to meet people because it's a lot easier to form friendships when you are 10 than at the age of 18 but eventually I struck out on my own and went to the liveliest local pub I could find.

I'd only been sitting at the bar for five minutes with a glass of wine when a guy bounded up to me, introduced himself as Johnny and told me he loved my long, straight black hair. He introduced me to his group of friends and I met loads of people of all ages. I was guarded about my past and told people I had just moved from Oxford but gave away no more than that. As soon as I mentioned I had a child the conversation was diverted and people wanted to know how old he was and what he was like.

Johnny was bubbly, fidgety and camp; he was lovely. He was 17 and after that first night we exchanged numbers and he was round my house practically every day afterwards. He was totally different to the kind of friends I'd had in the past; he was doing a course at a catering college. I started to consider my future too and decided to sign up to the same course. I wasn't necessarily interested in catering but I liked to cook and the course offered me the chance to expand my social circle.

Noah settled in well and I enrolled him at a local nursery, which he attended for less than a year before he went up to big school. The nursery mums were not so welcoming as I would have hoped, though. Mum was a lot older than many of them and I was a lot younger so we stuck out like an odd couple.

I also found people in the town could be judgemental. Oxford had been a multicultural city, where I had mixed with people from all races and religions without a second thought. Our new town was predominantly made up of white, middle-class elderly people.

I was on a bus into town one day and having a singalong with Noah when an elderly woman sitting on a seat opposite exclaimed, 'Not only is your son black, you are underage.'

Noah looked at me, then carried on singing but her words stung me: I was shocked. I had never experienced racism before with my son.

I glared at the woman.

'One, he is not black,' I said sternly. 'Two, I am not underage and, three, how dare you talk to me like that!'

The woman started ranting about how there are too many immigrants in this country and in the end the driver shouted to her and told her, if she didn't shut up, he would throw her off the bus.

After that incident I questioned whether it would have been better to have moved somewhere more multicultural for Noah's sake. When he moved into school, there were a couple of Asian and Oriental children but that was it. In his class he was the only mixed-race person but the pupils, mums and staff were brilliant with him and he loved school so I figured the most important thing was his happiness and comfort. He did look very different to the other children – he had big black curly hair and the staff made a huge deal about how handsome he was. They were also very understanding and non-judgemental about the situation surrounding his father. So many of the stories we read at a young age are all about Mum and Dad living happily together in a home and for many families that's just not the way it is. Noah did get confused sometimes but he was not the only child who didn't have contact with his dad. When asked where his daddy was, he explained that he didn't have a dad, he had a mummy and a granny instead.

Motherhood was harder because I was doing more and was more involved. All the time I was there being a normal mum, whereas before I was never there. I was learning and discovering what I had missed out on in Noah's early life. He fell ill with chicken pox and I felt like a real mum then because I was nursing him and comforting him, making sure he was OK. Then he started to respond to me as his mum. Previously, if I'd asked him to do something, he would ignore me and go and look at my mum for guidance. Mum and I worked together; we would discuss decisions and the partnership worked. She always asked me if I was happy with things before she said something to Noah. We developed mutual respect and we argued much less.

I didn't miss Oxford at all. I rarely went back but, when I did go back to visit friends, I kept my head down and away from places where the gang would be. Each time, I felt unsettled and anxious and I realised why I had got away. The city of dreaming spires looked like a dump – I didn't notice the beautiful architecture, I saw the people taking crack in the public toilets.

In my new life, I even tentatively started having a normal relationship. I met a lovely young man who was in the army. We started seeing each other after we met in town one night. Mum loved him and he was great with Noah. We went out on family trips and the relationship lasted several months. He was the only man who ever told me he loved me and meant it. But everything that had happened to me had an impact and while he was fantastic, I couldn't have a physical relationship with him. He didn't care and told me it didn't matter but, it did to me. It was everything I wanted but I just couldn't commit and in the end I told him I could only be his friend. He was upset and explained that he would wait for as long as I needed. We stayed friends.

Some wounds, I knew, would take a long time to heal.

Chapter twenty

OPERATION BULLFINCH

I did my best to try to forget the past and focused on my new life. But my past refused to forget me. In January 2012 I was at college and looking to the future. Everything seemed to be going in the right direction. Since moving I'd had a few problems settling in. At one point I'd briefly been on antidepressants and some days my past hung around my neck like a heavy millstone and weighed me down. But I tried hard not to think about it; I put it in a box and locked it away at the back of my mind and generally I was upbeat. I had the freedom to choose my own future and to make my own decisions.

And then Mum received a letter. It was sent jointly from Thames Valley Police and Oxford Social Services and asked if she would ask me whether I would agree to talk to a police officer about an investigation the force was conducting into alleged sexual exploitation. It mentioned nothing about suspects, witnesses, trials or charges; it was vague.

If I'm honest, had I known then that there would be a subsequent trial at which I would be a witness, I would not have agreed to get involved. At that point in my life I just wanted to move on and the psychological shackles the gang had placed on me remained strong; I was still scared. But all the letter asked for was an informal chat.

Mum said she would support any decision I made and so I agreed to meet them. Initially two people came from Oxford and explained that there was a task force investigating child sexual exploitation, in and around the town. They had noticed a pattern in many cases and records showed that my experiences might be related to the areas they were investigating. They asked if I would be happy to speak to a police officer. It was the first time that I started to get a definite idea that perhaps there had been more girls like me. While Mohammed had once asked me to be a recruiter and I saw other girls at the barbecue, I never got the impression it was widespread practice.

They didn't make it clear but at that point they were fishing to see who would be willing to supply evidence; they needed to build up the trust of the girls they thought might have been victims. Someone had seen a pattern and was linking past cases that were similar.

I agreed to speak further and the next person who came to see me was WPC Jane Crump. It was lovely to see her again and, away from the gang and with the confidence of a new life, I felt I could be more open with her.

'It'll just be an off-the-record statement,' she said. She didn't tell me anything about the investigation and explained that she was initially just looking for background information that might help them.

I started to speak about what had happened. Names came up that sent shivers down my spine: Mohammed Karrar, Bassam Karrar, Akhtar and Anjum Dogar. I blurted it all out and it felt good that finally someone was listening. Jane had always suspected that something bigger was happening in the city and finally her suspicions were being investigated. At that point no one mentioned the word 'trafficking'. I didn't know what that term meant until later in the process when someone said I was a 'trafficked person'.

After that meeting, Jane came down to see me on a regular basis. She is very loud and bubbly, and was easy to talk to. Slowly and skilfully she built up a picture of my life. All the while, I had no idea of the scope of the investigation. I told her about how Mohammed had befriended me, about the men, the trips to London, the drugs, the barbecues and the violence. I was convinced it was all my fault and that I had brought it on myself.

For about six weeks running, Jane came down once a week and took statements from me. We went deeper and deeper into the story. Every week she would turn up with her tape recorder; we would talk through events, she would go off and listen back and return with more questions she wanted answered. But I never felt under pressure and I felt that I could trust her. As the process expanded, my reservations melted away. It wasn't easy going back through the difficult details, but Jane made it easier. I discovered that it was easier to talk about it rather than keep it all in, and because of the sensitive nature of a lot of what I was telling her, it was easier to talk to Jane than to Mum.

I hoped that, by helping the police, I might be able to stop what had happened to me happening to someone else. There had been no mention of a trial and prosecutions. In my naïvety I assumed the purpose of the investigation was to prevent it from happening to other girls and to allow the authorities to spot the signs and identify victims. I wasn't aware of the huge effort that had been going on behind the scenes for several months before I was even contacted.

The foundations of 'Operation Bullfinch', as it was called, were laid a few months after I moved from Oxford in November 2010. One of the senior police officers in Oxford, a man called Simon Morton, had listened to what Jane had been saying and noted there was a pattern of young girls from similar backgrounds going missing from the city. When they returned, none of them was willing to speak to police or parents about what they had been doing or where they had been. He discovered that there was intelligence that suggested the girls were also mixing with older men.

It was the first time anyone in a senior position had decided to take a closer look at this pattern to see if there were links between the girls. Simon persuaded his superiors to allocate funds and manpower to the investigation and, in May 2011, a taskforce was set up, which consisted of ten officers and two social workers. The secondment of the social workers to the team allowed both agencies to share information.

The team looked at files relating to girls who had been classified as medium-risk mispers (missing persons), both past and present; girls like me, who had a history of disappearing for a few days at a time. When they reappeared an officer was always dispatched to interview them and the reports that were filed usually classed them as streetwise kids and troublemakers. There was also information suggesting that some of the girls were prostituting themselves and having sex with older men. The inference was that this was their own choice. Simon didn't believe any young girl would choose to sell herself of her own accord and wanted to know why these cases were happening. It was a difficult task because when the investigation was launched there were no complaints, no witnesses and no offenders.

The first girl who was interviewed had led a life very similar to mine: she came from a vulnerable background and had been a runaway in her early teens. She had never discussed fully what was happening to her at the time but had intimated that one day she would. She grew up, moved away and carved out a career for herself. As the team began to look into past case histories of potential victims, they came across her details and contacted her. She had not been in contact for six years but, when she spoke, her story mirrored what intelligence suggested was happening in the present. She gave details of the same pattern of abuse and gave the police the same names. The officers realised that the exploitation had been going on for many years.

The operation continued to widen and more past and present victims were identified.

The case needed to be watertight and so the officers carried out a range of different surveillance. Phones were monitored and the team worked secretly to gather evidence. The meticulous investigation had been leading up to what police called 'strike day' – the day when the addresses of all the suspects were raided.

Just before 6am on 22 March 2012, 14 addresses across Oxford were raided. There were 250 officers involved in the swoop and the 13 men arrested were suspected of crimes including rape and sex trafficking of girls aged between 11 and 15.

At the time of the arrests, no names were published but I knew the interviews I had given would have related to the raids and the investigation. The men were taken in for questioning. I watched the news nervously, waiting for updates and information. There was a time limit on how long the police could hold the men without charge and that limit was extended to allow them to be further questioned. During that period, WPC Jane Crump came down to see me again. There was very little she could say but she wanted more information and clarification. She explained that some people had been arrested who related to my statement but mentioned no names. I then realised the questioning was not solely about future prevention and protection of other girls going through what I had been through; it was about putting the men on trial. It was a jolt of realisation that frightened me – I worried for my safety and for the safety of Noah and Mum.

If Mohammed and Spider were in custody, I knew exactly what they were capable of doing if they were released and, despite the fact that there was a massive investigation in process, I still didn't have complete faith in the police and courts that they would be convicted. I was nervous and I told Jane. I didn't know there were other witnesses involved. The prospect that I would have to attend court and give evidence had not occurred to me; it was not something I relished.

Jane reassured me at this stage it was still uncertain whether I would be needed and, if I was, I would be afforded complete anonymity and protection. I still felt uncomfortable but agreed to continue co-operating with the investigation and gave an official statement that would be used as evidence in the case.

The police were allowed to hold the men for four days and in that time, as well as giving statements, I was asked to go to Abingdon police station, near Oxford, to do a video ID parade. I went on the train with Mum. At the station we were taken to a formal, bare room, where monitors had been set up. The room was full of solicitors representing the men in custody. They looked at me when I walked in and didn't say anything – they were there to observe me doing the ID parade. I was asked to look at four line-ups; there were nine men in each. I scanned the first. In the middle of the row stood Mohammed; he looked absolutely crazy – he was grinning, his eyes were wide and staring. He looked as if he had been on drugs. I picked him out immediately. In the following parades, I identified Bassam, Spider and Jammy. The two Dogar brothers were smiling. Bassam looked sheepish and confused, like he'd just been woken up.

I shivered as footage of each of the evil monsters played out in front of me. Each time I confirmed the identity of one of the men, a solicitor would get up and walk out.

I had to watch the short clips three times even though on each occasion I was certain on the first showing who was in the line-up.

Mum also had to identify Mohammed because he had threatened her. She had met him once when he was dealing drugs on the street.

I was quiet on the way home; the parade had shook me up. I hadn't seen those faces for a long time and I had thought that I'd left them behind in a previous life I wanted to forget. Yet there they were, staring out at me from a police station monitor, intimidating and crashing in on the new life I had made for myself.

A few days later Jane Crump called. She was shrieking down the phone.

'We've got them, we've got them!'

The men had been charged and among those who would face trial were Mohammed, Bassam, Spider and Jammy. I didn't know whether to be pleased or to be sick; my stomach lurched. Jane explained that I would be safe and that the men would most probably be held on remand because of the severity of the charges but still I feared for our safety. We were given a special panic alarm, which was linked directly to the police and ensured they would be at our house within minutes if it was activated. For the first time in over a year, I felt I had to look over my shoulder and I began to seriously doubt whether I had done the right thing. I had a nagging worry that the case would be dropped before it got to court or that the men would be found not guilty.

The charges were reported in the national press. I looked online and saw their mugshots on news websites: they looked like tramps. Over the following weeks I came to terms with my involvement, even though I didn't have faith that the court case would get very far or that the jury would believe us. I was hopeful, however, and, although the police could not give out too much information, they did reassure me that they had a strong case.

Even though the gang were remanded, I was worried that someone associated with them would find out where we were; the network they were associated with was vast. The reality of my involvement in the case set in and, in the following weeks, I lost grip of the optimism that I had painstakingly built. I found it exhausting to think about the details of the case and old feelings that I had moved on from long ago were dredged up. Sometimes I felt angry that I had become involved again; I suffered panic attacks, I became reclusive and, when I went out, I worried that people knew who I was and what I'd been involved in. I became paranoid. I also began arguing with Mum once again because, while I was reluctant, she was enthusiastic and ready for it all to happen. I wanted to forget all about it. She felt she had failed so much and needed to get justice to make up for her perceived failings.

'You never failed me, Mum,' I told her. 'You did everything you could possibly have done and more to protect me.'

As she was a witness in the trial, too, we weren't supposed to talk about what we had discussed with the police. I was also told that, because we were both involved, we would not be able to be together in court. Mum was my main support and the thought of going through cross-examination alone filled me with dread.

Mum still did not know the full details of what had happened to me and I couldn't warn her how graphic some of them would be.

'It is not going to be nice,' I tried to explain. 'You are going to hear some horrible things. You are going to hear things that will upset you.'

I don't think anything could have prepared her for the full details of the abuse. I still thought I was partly to blame and was worried about what she would think of me. She knew about the drugs but she didn't know the details of the sexual exploitation.

The psychological strain became immense. Some days I couldn't get out of bed, I felt so down and lethargic. I had no energy, I was tired all the time but I couldn't sleep. Some days I wouldn't eat, other times I would binge. I hadn't told any of my new circle of friends about the case and my previous life, so I had no one to talk to.

Eventually I realised I was becoming depressed and so I went to my GP. I was prescribed Sertraline tablets, which are antidepressants given for depression and anxiety. When I told the doctor some of the background as to why I was feeling the way I was, she gave me details of a local support organisation specialising in supporting the victims of sexual exploitation.

I called and a few days later had an appointment. Mum and I went along to meet a guy called Graham who worked there. I was nervous because he was a man but I needn't have worried; he was absolutely lovely. Middle-aged, he looked innocent and posh but had tattoos everywhere so I could tell there was another side to him and that he had probably been around a bit. I warmed to him straight away; he put me at ease and he listened. Graham explained that if I wanted to use the charity's services he would be my court support; he would try to make sure everything was as easy as it could be for Mum and me. He put my mind at rest and I felt I could tell him anything. After that we had several other meetings and he went into more depth about what I could expect and what he could help me with.

Graham was very easy to talk to – he always started by talking about something funny. He made discussing difficult subjects easy; he never interrupted. He explained what I could expect, both in the run-up and through the trial. Also, he arranged for a pre-trial visit to London to familiarise myself with the court and said he would accompany me on that. Graham was the interface between me and the justice process. He took the pressure off me so that I could concentrate on the task I was going to have to perform and, more importantly, he was in my corner and he became my friend.

The months passed and the case progressed through hearings and committals. Like cowards, the gang pleaded not guilty, which meant there would definitely be a trial and that me and any other witnesses the police had would have to give evidence and face cross-examination in court. Eventually the case was scheduled to be heard at the Old Bailey in London, the most famous criminal court in the country. It was obvious how big it was going to be and the national and local news followed the story closely.

I knew nothing about the legal process and then the day arrived for my pre-trial visit, which was like an induction day, where I would get to meet the witness support team and look around the parts of the court where I would be. I wanted to be reassured that I would not be visible to the rest of the courtroom.

I went on the visit with Mum, Graham and one of his colleagues, Eloise. We had arranged to meet WPC Jane Crump in London, in a cafe near the Old Bailey.

When we did, she was with another woman who none of us had met before. Jane introduced her: she was from Oxford Social Services.

I was furious.

'What is she doing here?' I said. I hadn't heard from social services for years and both Mum and I had a deep-seated mistrust of social workers. The last run-in I had with them was when I thought they were going to take Noah away from me and I wrongly assumed that was why she was there: because there was concern for Noah due to the case.

'Get her out,' I demanded. 'I'm not doing anything if she's here!'

It wasn't the woman's fault: she was just doing her job and was there because Oxford Social Services had been involved in Operation Bullfinch. But given my history with social services I should have been pre-warned. I'm afraid I was openly hostile to her and it must have been a very uncomfortable afternoon for her.

We walked from the cafe to the court and were guided around the building; we were shown a courtroom and shown behind the scenes. We were taken to where I would enter the building and I was shown that it was secluded and that I could not be seen by people. I was shown around the area where the witnesses wait to be called and was taken into a courtroom similar to the one I would give evidence in.

The Old Bailey was a big scary building; it felt like there was lots of nasty history there. I sat in one of the docks where the defendants sit and tried to imagine how they would be feeling; I hoped they would be as scared as I had been for many years.

'How strong is the door?' I asked a guide.

She locked it.

'Try it,' she said.

I shook and rattled the door and leaned all my weight against it; it wouldn't budge. Now I was satisfied none of the men would be able to break out.

The guide showed me the public gallery, which was above the courtroom. I was worried someone would be able to jump over and get to me. She explained that if there was any danger the front section of the gallery would be closed off and assured me that no one in the gallery would be able to see me.

The visit lasted for four hours. It was close to Christmas so afterwards we went to Oxford Street to see the lights and then we went to Selfridges and had some wine.

It took another six months before the trial started. All during that time, I worried. The police did everything they could to make the experience comfortable; they even hired a safe house in London near the court for the witnesses to stay in while we gave evidence. I knew that I had no real choice and that if I decided not to give evidence then I would have been summoned anyway. It took almost a year between the gang being charged and the case coming to court; they were on remand all that time. Throughout that year, I had to give loads of statements. I saw the police frequently and had to relive many difficult memories. Sometimes I went over the same thing again and again as they built the case.

I knew there were six girls who were victims and I thought that one of the girls may have been someone I knew from Oxford because I had been asked about her.

In relation to crimes against me, Spider, Jammy and Mohammed were charged with conspiracy to rape. The Dogar brothers were further charged with trafficking me for sexual exploitation and facilitating child prostitution. Bassam was charged with rape. They also faced many charges in relation to the other girls.

I heard about a similar case in Rochdale but I didn't watch the news and didn't make the link between that case and mine. After the case was over I learned that, although the suspects were different, the method was the same. There, girls had been groomed and passed around between older men for sex. Nine men were convicted in that case, which took place in May 2012, two months after the gang had been arrested.

Chapter twenty-one
THE TRIAL

I was 'girl three' in the line-up of victims; the third to give evidence. I wasn't needed at the beginning of the case while the first two victims gave their evidence and so I stayed at home until I was summoned.

One of the girls before me admitted to lying and the man she was testifying against was let off – that was a big setback. Once girl two finished, I was alerted. I was asked to travel to London on a Wednesday and I was due to give evidence the next day. Halfway there, I was told there were some legal technicalities that needed to be dealt with and that I would have to wait another day. Noah was staying with his auntie (I had told him that I had to go away for a few days to help a judge tell off some naughty men) and he was excited about staying away for a few days because he knew he would be pampered. As Mum and I were on the way we carried on and went to the safe house, where there were two police officers staying to look after us. Both girl one and girl two had stayed in the house while they were in court (once each girl had finished giving her evidence she moved out to make way for the next witness). The police officers were supposed to make us feel secure. They made me more nervous, however, because their presence reminded me that I was at risk.

Several months before the trial I had stopped the catering course I was on and I wasn't working. There was no way I could have been employed, I was a wreck. Constantly shaking, I suffered anxiety attacks and depression. I couldn't focus and my life was in limbo while I waited. I told the college that I was about to be a witness in a trial but didn't go into detail. Once again, a part of my life and education remained unfinished and incomplete because of the men. The investigation and case had taken up over a year of my life.

The safe house was in a lovely part of North London called Hampstead. Eloise and Graham were also with us. We arrived in the evening and as the police officers stationed there were making their dinner in the kitchen we went to a fish and chip shop for supper. It was an easy night and we had a laugh.

I had a chest infection at the time and didn't sleep well because I was coughing. Lying awake, I tried to picture what it was going to be like in court the following day. When I eventually did drift off to sleep, I had an awful dream that Mohammed had phoned me.

The following morning I got up and went downstairs in my pyjamas to make a coffee. There was a strange man and woman slouched on the sofa, empty bags of crisps and a takeaway pizza box on the couch. They said hello and introduced themselves as police officers (they had swapped shifts in the middle of the night). I was unsettled by the idea of waking up with strangers in the house. Mum agreed and we requested a change in the living arrangements. The police officers were removed and stationed in a hotel just down the road.

After breakfast, as I was psyching myself up for my first day in court, the message came through that I was not needed that day. But I had got used to the way the justice system worked and was annoyed but not surprised. I used the extra day to get a doctor's appointment at a walk-in centre and got some medicine for my chest.

That night I Skyped Noah and it was lovely to see his happy face. I blinked back the tears and put on a brave smile. It had only been a day but I missed him and, even though I was allowed to see him at the weekend, I didn't know how long I was going to be in London. Undoubtedly my evidence would run over into the following week.

'Has the judge got those bad men yet, Mummy?' he asked.

'Not yet, darling, but don't worry – he will,' I told him.

By Thursday night, I knew that whatever had prevented me from starting that morning had been dealt with and that I would be in court the following morning. Finally, it was real – it was going to happen. That night we all went to Pizza Express but I didn't have much of an appetite. Subdued and withdrawn, I was lost in my thoughts and nerves.

The following morning, after a fitful night's sleep, I woke and was absolutely terrified. I felt sick and chain-smoked to try to calm my nerves. The stress of the last year seemed to have concentrated into a ball and lodged itself in my stomach.

Perhaps deep down I thought it would never happen because the case had been postponed so many times. Graham tried to calm me down and I could see that Mum was nervous too. I was physically sick several times.

'Lara, you have to eat, you will need to keep your energy up,' Graham fussed. I had no appetite but he forced me to eat a single piece of toast.

Several weeks before, I had gone shopping with Mum to buy an outfit for court. I didn't need to be briefed about clothes. I knew I should dress smartly and I picked a black suit, which I wore over a brightly coloured top. My fingers shook as I did up the buttons on the jacket. I wore my hair up and minimal make-up.

At 8.20am we got a call from the two police officers who were taking us to the court, informing us they were outside.

'I can't go!' I sobbed to Graham.

'Yes, you can,' he answered sternly. Like a little girl I stood in the corner of the room, terrified of what lay ahead. I was shaking as he gently led me out.

The car was a big saloon with blacked-out windows and the men driving it were close protection officers named Paul and Ollie. They explained that they had guarded the Prime Minister and the Queen so I had no need to worry and they were so lovely, they eased my nerves.

We drove purposefully across the city – we needed to be at our destination in plenty of time. At one point a woman driver cut in front of the car and forced us to stop suddenly. My heart lurched and, when Paul sounded the horn, she turned around and started to remonstrate, flashing him her middle finger. In response he flashed her his warrant card.

'You've got a finger, I've got one of these,' he said.

Sheepishly she turned round and drove off carefully.

When we turned a corner and I saw the Old Bailey in front of us I nearly passed out with nerves. I could feel my heart pounding in my chest; I gripped Mum's hand tightly.

We drove around the side of the court complex and up to a large iron gate: it felt like we were going into a prison. A head popped out from a small opening next to the gate as we approached. It belonged to one of the guards, who checked to make sure we were an authorised vehicle. We slowed but before we stopped the huge doors slid open and we glided in and down a concrete ramp, which led into the car park. We parked directly in front of a door, which was opened for us by an usher as the car stopped. Ollie told us to get out and to keep our backs to the gates, which were sliding back shut so no one outside on the street could see our faces.

Once outside we bundled through the door and into a small lift, which whizzed us up to the Witness Services section of the court – a secure area where witnesses wait and where all the witness staff are located. From approaching the court to stepping out of the lift took just seconds and was swift and slick. It was impressive and would have been exciting had I not been so terrified of what lay ahead.

Every effort was made to make witnesses feel comfortable. There were staff on hand to offer an endless supply of tea and coffee; there was a kitchen, toilets and a lounge with a television inside. I couldn't relax, though – I was having serious doubts.

As I waited, I felt waves of nausea and had to stick my head out of a window to gasp in a lungful of fresh air and stop myself from being sick again. Mum and Graham kept trying to force me to eat sandwiches. Paul and Ollie were assigned to be with me throughout and they followed me everywhere, even outside when I went out for a cigarette.

I spoke to WPC Jane Crump, who told me things looked positive because of the defence the gang had come up with. To counter the charges relating to me, Mohammed was claiming that I had forced him to take drugs and made him have sex with me when we first met when I was 13. I laughed when I heard this. How was anyone going to believe that? But it was all he could come up with and the others were going to say similar things: that I had forced and threatened them, and that I was a ringleader.

After two hours, I was called to the courtroom.

Before I left, I gave myself a pep talk. The men were sick and depraved, they had no respect and what they had done to me was wrong. They deserved to face justice and that's what I told myself as I made my way to the courtroom.

Walking to the witness box was terrifying: I had to walk through the courtroom where there were boards in place forming a corridor to protect me from seeing the defendants and to obscure me from the public gallery. I could hear the hubbub of the court before I climbed up into the witness box. When I got there, I looked out and saw people everywhere. The room was packed and it felt intimidating. I looked across to the Judge's bench and Judge Peter Rook looked at me and smiled in his red robes and white wig. Just in front of him sat the defence barristers. They looked like a pack of wolves and I decided not to focus on them. I looked at the jury and decided to keep my attention on them as they looked friendlier than anyone else. There was a black lady with an afro sitting in the jury and she reminded me of my son. She had a kind face and also looked at me and smiled. I realised then they were all humans with hearts while the barristers were obviously not and were instead preparing to rip me apart with their cross-examination.

Next to the witness box was the dock where all the defendants were lined up. There was supposed to be a curtain pulled across the partition between the witness box and the dock to spare me from having to look at the ugly faces lined up inside it. It wasn't pulled back far enough, however, and, as soon as I walked in to sit down, I got a full view of the men on trial. I saw Mohammed sitting back casually, looking up at the ceiling. Panicked, I jumped backwards to get out of their line of vision. As I did so, I knocked into the usher who had shown me to my place. Another usher came running across the room and pulled the curtain closed. I stood still and breathed deeply before I sat down.

The first stage in my evidence was cross-examination by the prosecution solicitor. He was basically on my side and it was his job to ask me about all the details of the case. His name was Noel Lucas. He was in his fifties and broad, he wore a white wig and a black gown and to me he looked like

Mr Toad from *Wind in the Willows*. His questioning was not confrontational. It was his job to ask me questions that would allow me to tell my story. He let it be known that if, at any point, I felt it was all too much then I could stop. This point was reiterated by the judge.

'I am going to ask you a few questions about the horrific abuse you suffered at the hands of these defendants,' said Noel, gesturing towards the men behind the curtain. 'Is that OK with you, Lara?'

'Yes,' I said as clearly as my nerves would allow.

Noel started by talking to me about my early life and about when I met Mum. He described my life with my birth parents as a very abusive, neglectful background and explained that when I first moved to Oxford I was a relatively normal and happy child who had come from a difficult background. Then he described how I had met Mohammed and asked me questions about the months leading up to when he gave me drugs. I had to go through my statements and relate them to each defendant. Then I was given a folder full of evidence: it was awful because it contained pictures of me that I had forgotten about. There were photographs of me when I first met the gang; I was just a child and, when I looked at them, I was overcome with anger and sadness because I realised what the men had stolen from that poor innocent girl in the pictures. There were also photographs taken of the injuries I'd sustained after Bassam raped and assaulted me.

I was made to relive all the events – the rape, the trafficking, the barbecues, the heroin overdose. As each shocking detail was introduced, I felt myself get stronger. It was the first time I had ever been given the opportunity to tell my side of the story in public and gradually I felt a weight lifting from me. I spoke up when I answered the questions because I wanted the men to hear what they had done to me; it was a horrific list of abuse. I wanted the court to know what had happened to me, and what the suspects were capable of.

At certain points there were gasps from the jury, particularly when details were given about the rape in the Nanford. At one point, I looked at the jurors and one of the men in the front row was crying. I was very open and honest – I explained that I was no angel and that I had been vile to my mum, I was abusive and aggressive. I admitted I did drugs in the past, but explained that still did not excuse what was done to me.

Occasionally the proceedings were adjourned, usually after an objection from one of the defence barristers. There were so many tactics in play that I wasn't aware of. Both sides would have done deals about what questions could and couldn't be asked, what would and wouldn't be challenged, and each time there was an adjournment I assumed some other deal was being struck. At points it seemed choreographed – they flounced around theatrically in their gowns. After Noel had talked me through my evidence, he handed me over to the prosecution. There were nine men in the dock and my evidence directly related to five of them, which meant I was cross-examined by five different defence QCs. The men were Bassam, Anjam, Mohammed, Ahktar and another man, who was eventually convicted of two counts of sexual activity with a child but not for offences relating to me. The first was very simple: I was only asked whether I was sure the person I had given evidence about was the person in court. I confirmed it was.

After the first day I was confident I had given a good account of myself. Court finished and I went back to the safe house for the night and then travelled home to see Noah the following day. He had laid out the table like a restaurant and made a sign above it. We had a big roast dinner together and talked about normal family stuff – it felt good to put the case to one side and get on with normal life. I was needed in court on the Monday so the following afternoon I had to leave again but it was hard to tear myself away from my son. He was very stand-offish and I couldn't blame him. I told myself that, once the trial had finished, I would be able to start my life properly.

'Mummy will be back soon and I promise I won't go away again after that,' I soothed him. He didn't say anything but his body language said it all.

Paul and Ollie came to collect me and drove Graham and me back to London. Mum stayed home for an extra day. We decided it would be better for Noah to have her there for as long as possible. I psyched myself up for more of the defence case – I knew it wasn't all going to be an easy ride. Mohammed and Bassam were both out to try to ruin my reputation. I slept fitfully only to be told the following morning that I wouldn't be needed that day after all. I had a day to kick around and think about things so Graham decided to arrange something to take my mind off things.

'Let's go and get tattoos,' he suggested.

I laughed. He was covered in them. I'd had a couple over the years but wasn't against having any more.

'I don't know...' I hesitated.

'Come on,' he said. 'It'll mark the end of something and the start of your new life.'

I agreed and called Mum to tell her about the plan. She reluctantly agreed and suggested that perhaps I should have a design with a barrister's wig with an arrow through it. Instead, I had a butterfly to signify freedom from the past and transformation.

Mum came back down that night with her brother, Michael, and we went to a lovely fish restaurant for dinner.

The difficult cross-examination began in earnest the next day when the defence tried to discredit me and trash Mum. They asked me leading questions about her and the boundaries she set for me, and tried to imply that she had let me run off and was too lenient.

I got angry.

'She worked bloody hard to get me safe, don't you dare try and blame her!' I shot back.

They said that I obviously wasn't close to her, otherwise I wouldn't have behaved in the way I did. Then they started to question my relationship with Noah. I knew they were trying to unsettle me and so I did my best to stay calm but I was still very annoyed.

I got strength when I looked over at the jury and saw their faces. They looked just as appalled as I was at the line of questioning.

At one stage, I was speaking about Spider, explaining he was an evil man and that I wasn't scared of him anymore. Suddenly, I heard raised voices and banging. It sounded like something was happening in the dock. Adrenaline surged through me. I looked over at the judge and saw him jump up from his seat. Then I heard movement and so I panicked – I thought someone was coming to get me. I couldn't see the dock or the public gallery. I stood up and bolted out the door behind me, clattering into the witness services lady who was with me.

'It's OK, calm down,' she said as she held my shoulders. 'It's in the court next door – it's safe in here.'

But I was petrified and shaking. Some sort of commotion had broken out in the adjoining room. I had to take a short break to calm my nerves.

The defence took three days and it was exhausting; the barristers asked question after question. Several of them asked the same questions as the ones before. But each night I felt stronger and tried not to dwell on the events of the day. We had a meal or we watched a film in the house and tried to keep things as normal as we could.

In court I wasn't scared of the gang anymore. When I heard their defences I thought they were pathetic. Hearing the ridiculous stories they came up with made me realise just how weak they were and what cowards they were for putting me and the other victims through the ordeal of a trial. Halfway through I had the urge to take the curtains down and look at them.

In the witness box, I could hear them. They were about 10ft away and they coughed and fidgeted.

Mohammed's barrister was a woman and she implied that I was a racist because all the defendants were Muslims. It was a laughable claim: after all, I had a mixed-race son.

Bassam's defence barrister was a man called Mark Milliken-Smith. I don't care if I never see him again. He questioned me about the rape and tried to contest that I had lied about it, despite the recording of the phone call to the police from the man who had heard the attack that was played in court and the pictures of my injuries. He constantly brought up the fact that I had dropped the case; he became provocative and suggested Bassam couldn't have raped me because he couldn't get an erection, even though his DNA was there.

'I suggest you were telling lie upon lie because you'd been caught by police naked in a hotel room with a man you were not supposed to be with. At no stage were you struck by him at all. That is a lie. You were not punched to the face or body,' he pushed.

'No, that's a lie,' I argued.

'Not at any stage did he threaten you that he was going to kill you, or words to that effect? You cried rape, didn't you?'

'I didn't cry rape. I was raped,' I told the court.

I kept crying; it was excruciatingly uncomfortable.

Being called a liar when I knew I was right and the details were true was hard. Everything was thrown at me. At one stage, my commitment to Noah was called into question and it was suggested I didn't care for him.

I stood.

'Do you really think it is that easy for me to stand here and admit to you all that I don't know how many drugs I have done and how many people I have had sex with?' I stated.

The defence closed with Bassam and the last thing Milliken-Smith uttered was that he hoped he hadn't upset me.

The judge then said, 'You may go now,' and that was it; the ordeal was over. I breathed a sigh of relief and left the court.

Mum's evidence was equally compelling. Carefully, and eloquently, she explained about the fears she had had every time I went missing. She was always scared someone would call to inform her I was dead. She explained that she had lived with the constant thought that one day she would have to identify my body before she even got to know me. No one had any idea what she went through, least of all me.

My evidence gave way to girl four and I followed the case online when I returned home and tried to get on with my life. It became obvious to me straight away that she was my friend from Oxford. The confirmation that she had been involved hit me hard. She too was groomed and sold by Mohammed but she had it worse than anyone: her abuse began when she was 11. She had been branded with a hot iron by Mohammed so people would know she belonged to him. She was raped by Mohammed and Bassam and forced to be gang raped. When she was 12, Mohammed had got her pregnant and had taken her to a backstreet clinic for an illegal abortion. Her treatment was horrific. She was a good friend for a long time but I had no idea it was happening to her, too – I had never seen her with any of the men. Out of everything that happened at the trial that was the most upsetting of all, finding out the details of what one of my closest friends had been through. She had moved away when I went to the secure unit and we had lost contact; she gave evidence by video link.

Three weeks after I gave evidence the case ended. Everyone on the prosecution team was confident there would be convictions. The case against the men was strong and the evidence from each of us girls had been compelling and harrowing. There was no denying the same pattern had been followed each time: we had all come from similar backgrounds, we had been befriended, manipulated and brainwashed before being abused repeatedly and violently.

Once the case was wrapped up and the jury sent out, Mum scanned the internet constantly for news. We knew that after 3.30pm each day we were unlikely to hear as the court shut at that time. We were advised by the police to arrange a safe place we could go to at short notice once the verdict had been delivered, as there was a possibility that we would be approached by journalists and of reprisals because of the sensitive nature of the case. Some reporters had already been to the house and Mum had seen them off – I don't know how they got our address. I was warned it could take weeks to reach a verdict but in reality it took the jury just two and a half days to reach a decision.

It was late afternoon on 14 March 2013 and after hearing nothing all day I took the dogs for a walk and left my phone at home. I'd been out for some time and when I got home Mum practically fell on me when I walked through the door.

She was breathless.

'Where have you been? I thought you'd been kidnapped!'

'What are you talking about?' I asked, confused.

'They're guilty, all of them!' she shrieked.

'Who?' I frowned.

'The men, they've all been found guilty!'

I screamed and jumped up and down. We hugged, laughed and cried. I felt ecstatic – they had been found guilty on all charges.

Akhtar Dogar, 32, of Tawney Street, Oxford, was found guilty of five counts of rape, three counts of conspiracy to rape, two counts of child prostitution and one count of trafficking. Anjum Dogar, 31, of Tawney Street, Oxford, was found guilty of three counts of rape, two counts of child prostitution, three counts of conspiracy to rape and one count of trafficking. Mohammed Karrar, 38, of Kames Close, Oxford, was found guilty of two counts of conspiracy to rape, four counts of rape of a child, one count of using an instrument to procure miscarriage, two counts of trafficking, one count of assault of a child by penetration, two counts of child prostitution, three counts of rape, two counts of conspiracy to rape a child and one count of supplying a Class A drug. Bassam Karrar, 33, of Hundred Acres Close, Oxford, was found guilty of two counts of rape, one count of rape of a child, two counts of conspiracy to rape a child, two counts of child prostitution, one count of trafficking and one count of conspiracy to rape.

Two other men, also part of the gang, were convicted. One was found guilty of two counts of sexual activity with a child and the other was found guilty of five counts of rape, two counts of conspiracy to rape and one count of arranging child prostitution.

We barely had time to collect our thoughts before we realised we needed to leave the house. I was caught between the jubilation of the verdict and the worry that once again I had to take Noah away from his home to protect him. Although the men were now safely behind bars until their sentencing, their actions still cast a shadow over my life.

We went away for two nights and had the rolling news on as we watched the details being covered. Again and again the bulletins showed mugshots of the men.

In between the case closing and the verdict I had done an anonymous interview with the BBC and that night I went to the Co-op to buy a bottle of champagne to celebrate. The radio was on in the shop and my interview was being broadcast; it was surreal and unsettling. As I handed over the money I didn't speak in case the cashier recognised my voice.

I put Noah to bed as normal and told him that we had to go away for a few days because the judge had got the bad men – he seemed pleased. Then I got tipsy with Mum. We cried, we laughed as we watched the news and then I went to bed.

Sentencing was three weeks later and during that time I got on with my life. I tried not to think about what the men would get. I would have been disappointed if it were only a few months but for me the triumph was that they had been found guilty and that, finally, it was acknowledged that a grave wrong had been done to me.

There were all kinds of recriminations brewing. The police came under criticism for not doing enough to investigate the crimes as and when they were happening and Oxford Council came under massive criticism for not doing enough. A serious case review was ordered and there were calls for resignations.

I went along to see the men being sentenced because I wanted closure. The Old Bailey was packed and the hearing needed two courtrooms because there had been so many people involved in the trial. There were barristers, police officers and journalists; the public gallery was full. I sat next to the dock in between Mum and WPC Jane Crump.

Disappointingly, Mohammed wasn't there – he was too cowardly to come out of his cell. It's a shame he was allowed to hide away. I would have liked to have seen the look on his face when he realised how long he was going to be sent down for. Sentencing took about an hour and a half. The judge went through every charge, every girl's statement and every parent's statement. People were crying as he read out the details.

As the sentences were read out Jane squeezed my hand so tight, I thought she was going to break it.

Judge Rook told the men they had committed 'exceptionally grave crimes' and that the depravity they had shown was extreme. He praised us witnesses for our courage in giving evidence. Then he told the men: 'There can be no doubt that you have blighted lives and robbed them of their adolescence.

'Each of the six young girls has shown enormous courage in coming to the Old Bailey to give evidence, knowing they would be accused of lying, knowing they would have to relive their ordeals and knowing they have not been believed before. The jury has found they have come to the court to tell the truth.'

Akhtar and Anjum were both given life sentences and were told they would serve a minimum of 17 years each before being considered for release. I had to double-check I had heard correctly. As sentence was passed on Mohammed and Bassam, I held my breath: they were also given life sentences. Mohammed was told he would serve a minimum of 20 years and Bassam 15 years before they would be considered for release.

As the judge told the guards to take the men to their cells, one of them started sarcastically clapping. I didn't see who.

Speechless, I sat for a minute trying to take in what had happened. I had no idea the sentences would be so long. Eventually I was roused from what must have been shock by the movement of those around me who were getting up to walk out. Many had tears in their eyes. I thought Jane was going to burst with pride, she was so pleased – it was a phenomenal result. Like a herd of sheep we were led out and surrounded by police. Outside I was approached by a German journalist who was part of the press throng but one of the witness support workers came and told me not to talk.

After a debrief and congratulations from Noel, Mum and me went to the pub with the police. As we walked away from the courtroom there were press vans everywhere and reporters speaking urgently to cameras.

The atmosphere in the pub was wonderful. The police were all laid-back and relieved that they had got the right result. They had put so much time and effort into the investigation. I felt like part of a team, like we had all done it together; I felt safe and special. In the background there was a TV screen showing footage from outside the court. Then it cut to mugshots of the men. Mohammed's face flashed up, then Jammy, Spider and Bassam. Underneath each one, a caption gave details of their sentence. I looked at them without fear. I despised them all and what they had done, and as I took a sip of the champagne that was being handed out, I wished them as difficult and painful a sentence as they had handed out to me.

'Good riddance,' I whispered under my breath.

Epilogue

BLAMELESS

The story was in every newspaper and on every television station. It was one of the most controversial cases of sexual exploitation in British history. The nation was sickened by what had happened and the verdicts and sentences sparked reviews in authorities and agencies all over the UK. The one question that was continually asked was how had it happened on such a scale for so long?

Until the judge read out the sentences and sent the gang down for life I did not realise the scale of what I had been involved in. All the girls told the same story. We had been kept isolated so none of us realised there were others involved. And we were just the tip of the iceberg. Oxford police are still identifying victims – and that's just in one town.

The Children's Commissioner for England carried out a two-year study into child sexual exploitation by groups and gangs and issued a report in the wake of the Oxford case in November 2013. It identified several thousand children at risk of sexual exploitation by groups and gangs. The network of men I was sold to was vast: it was a factory that took in the vulnerable as raw material, corrupted them and put them to work. It is a grotesque industry and, sadly, I believe that it is just as prevalent now as it was when I myself was caught up in it.

The level of manipulation and coercion was shocking. Me and the other girls were brainwashed so effectively and thoroughly that none of us possessed free will. We were owned, we were hollow husks – our will belonged to the men. Singled out and isolated, we did not engage with anyone. The links we built with our abusers were based on a web of threats, addiction and compulsion. It was like Stockholm syndrome – the psychological phenomenon whereby victims of kidnapping start to display positive attachment to their captors. None of us was capable of making decisions for ourselves and were made to believe that what we were doing we were doing willingly. The men are paedophiles who are experts in grooming vulnerable girls. They are pieces of dirt who deserve nothing; they are weak and pathetic and the only solace I have is that they are the ones whose lives are over because they are locked away in cells.

It was only after I broke away from the gang that I began to realise the deep psychological control they had exerted over me. I had believed what happened to me was my own fault; I didn't see myself as a victim. Often I had felt a duty to protect them. They made me feel that I was the problem and I deserved to be treated the way I was, which I now know was ridiculous. I only really came to terms with the fact I wasn't to blame when I heard the details given at the trial – it was like a veil was lifted from my eyes.

I had always known that I had been let down by social services. At the height of my problems no one seemed to want to take control. But I'd been let down by them all my life, from their reluctance to act when I lived with Terri and Shane to the inappropriate placements they shuttled me between. However, I didn't realise just how much Mum had been let down by them too until I heard the evidence at the trial. While I was preoccupied with what was happening to me, she was desperately trying to make people aware that there was something very serious happening. Thankfully, things are changing. Local authorities are now re-evaluating the way they deal with children who go missing and who display signs of being exploited.

After things died down I tried to restart life once again but it has been hard. Meanwhile, Operation Bullfinch rumbled on and there were further arrests as the net widened. It became the highest priority for Oxford police, which meant there was the constant possibility I would have to give more statements. It was tiring; I just wanted to move on.

Soon after the sentencing I began to get depressed again. I have probably had depression for most of my life and now recognise that it builds up and comes to the surface when I don't have anything to occupy my mind. The trial and the run-up to it had taken so much time and energy, when it was over I felt deflated – I had no focus, I felt worthless. Lethargic, I didn't want to go out or talk to anyone so I went back to my GP, who prescribed antidepressants.

The psychological impact will probably be with me all my life. I had nightmares and flashbacks and needed sleeping tablets. I woke up screaming and Noah worried because he slept in the room opposite mine. Sometimes I woke up crying.

I tried to put everything behind me. If I thought too much about it then I started to get scared. Mum had nightmares too.

For a long time after the trial people who knew me were congratulating me.

'I bet you are happy?' they'd say.

Not really, I'd think, because they only got what they deserved and it still hasn't changed what happened, and is still happening.

I dealt with things my own way. I tried not to reflect and put everything to the back of my mind. To some extent I still do but eventually that will change, I expect. I no longer blame myself, which I did for a long time so I guess that's progress. And writing this book has helped me to make sense of it all and put events into perspective. Now that it's down on paper I'm hoping I can move on. I never had much faith in counsellors and haven't used them. And I wanted to leave a record for Noah so he knows the truth.

I am prepared for his questions when he is older. I expect he will be angry – he has every right to be. I will be blamed. I will tell him the truth and it will be his choice if he wants to find his father. If he does, I will help him. I don't know where Chris is now and do not want to know. But I would never stop Noah and I will warn him that he will be let down by either of the men who may have fathered him.

The biggest confidence booster I had after the trial was getting my first job in the summer of that year. I was convinced I was unemployable because my education had been so chequered and I'd been in trouble with the police. But Mum kept encouraging me and so I went to the job centre. I applied for a job in a care home, waited for months and heard nothing. I got despondent and wrote it off but then out of the blue I received a letter in the post saying I had been invited for a job interview out of 170 applicants. I convinced myself there and then that I would get let down but I went for the interview and, when they called me an hour later and offered me the job, I was ecstatic. A few weeks later I started the job. I loved it and the sense of worth it gave me – I got a real buzz from earning my own money and being able to look after my son and buy him things. I'm determined to give him a better start in life than the one I had.

I love him, and so does his granny.

When I look back at those first 10 years of my life before I was adopted it seems like they were lived by another person. And so they were: they belong to Lauren, not Lara. Now I have my little boy I realise how important love, security and boundaries are. That lack of love and care when I was growing up did affect me and my siblings. It affected the way we were to each other in the end – we started to change towards each other because we didn't know what love is. Our relationships since have been difficult and we've all faced our own issues. My siblings aren't regularly in my life anymore, which is sad. I see them now and then. Jayden looks after Nan and

Granddad, and the last time I saw Shane was when I was 18 – I don't wish to see him again.

I have family and he is not part of it. And to my family I owe everything. If it wasn't for Noah, I would be dead. Having him helped me to see things for what they were and I hope I earn the title of Mum from him. Mum's love and persistence also saved me. She persevered with me, and with trying to bring awareness to what was happening.

I've discovered I am a strong person – I'm going to get on with my life and I'm not going to let what happened hold me back. Now my bad days are cheered up by my little boy coming home and making me smile and telling me how his day went, or my mum taking the mickey out of me and telling me to stop being so grumpy.

I want a normal life. That's how I want to be seen, not as 'girl three' but as a normal girl.

The impact on my personal life will take a long time to heal. I'm still not ready for a relationship. I can't be touched intimately, even by a doctor. I am still trying to focus my mind on what is normal, healthy behaviour and what is wrong and inappropriate. It will take time to reset those parameters because they have been so corrupted. I'd love another child in the future but I can't bear to be touched and I don't see marriage as being for me. My past would be a lot for a man to cope with. Hopefully though, I'll get there with relationships; I am still young. My priority is work and my son. I want him to grow into a happy, healthy and proud little boy. I want him to be proud of himself, where he comes from, and to be proud of me, his mum.

Sometimes I can't believe everything that has happened. I walk down the street with Mum or I pick Noah up from school and I'm just another young mum trying to get on with her life as best she can. But I've been part of a world that most people cannot understand; I've seen things and been to dark places that defy comprehension. I can spot the telltale signs of abuse a mile off. Sometimes I'll be walking down the street or sitting on the bus and will pick up on a subtle cue and it jars my world in the same way as my own world of drug dealers and pimps barged into Mum's cosy life when I first became entangled in it.

Recently I was in McDonald's and I saw a young girl sitting with an older man. He was probably her grandfather or uncle. I could tell by her body language that she was uncomfortable. He was overly tactile and she was pulling away from his touch. When he handed her a Happy Meal, his hand hovered for too long over her backside. It turned my stomach. To anyone else it might have looked innocent but to me it was revolting because I knew it suggested abuse.

Mum has used her experiences for good and now advises agencies on what to look for in cases of abuse and exploitation. Telltale signs are excessive drinking and drug use, dressing in age-inappropriate clothing, denial and aversion to affectionate gestures. She teaches people not to assume that just because someone says they are OK, then they are OK.

The case opened up a lot of issues about race and religion because the defendants were Muslim. Whatever their beliefs, they still committed horrific crimes and I don't believe the issue should be ignored just because it is sensitive. While there are paedophiles in every race and religion, I do think the gang behaved in the way they did because of cultural differences in how they viewed women. Statistically there are more white male paedophiles but the structured gang set-up seems to be something to do with Muslim men and I think that stems from a lack of respect for women with a certain section of men. In my experience some British-born Muslim young men, particularly in Cowley, had no respect for women.

For the victims life has been a struggle. I'm one of the lucky ones – I have a job, a mum who is devoted and loving, and a son to live for. Most days I am positive about the future. Most of the other girls are piecing their lives back together. Sadly there are a couple who are stuck at a crossroads and that is sad – they don't feel they have anything to live for. Hopefully, this will change.

I took the decision to write this book and tell my story because I am blameless and I have nothing to hide. I'm proud of who I am, and I'm proud to have made a stand.

Now I have a life to get on with.

Acknowledgements

Thank you to my wonderful mum for giving me the opportunity to be who I am and for sticking by me and believing in me.

Thank you to my family and friends for your support. Thank you, Jane Crump, for working so hard for justice for all the girls and to Simon Morton for your determination.

Thanks to all at Ebury Publishing for giving me the opportunity to tell my story.

Thank you to Nick Harding for your help and guidance.